Isaac Hogarth is a barrister at 12 King's Bench Walk, specialising in clinical negligence and personal injury law. Isaac has a special interest in claims involving sepsis and meningitis. His experience includes appearing for bereaved families at inquests where the deceased has died from sepsis in a hospital setting. He has also given seminars on sepsis and meningitis claims.

Before coming to the Bar, Isaac worked in the clinical negligence department of a leading firm of solicitors. He is married to a paediatrician.

# A Practical Guide to Sepsis and Meningitis Claims

# A Practical Guide to Sepsis and Meningitis Claims

Isaac Hogarth
MA (Oxon)
Barrister
12 King's Bench Walk, London

Law Brief Publishing

Published 2019 by Law Brief Publishing, an imprint of Law Brief Publishing Ltd
30 The Parks
Minehead
Somerset
TA24 8BT

www.lawbriefpublishing.com

Paperback: 978-1-912687-29-9

*For Joshua*

# PREFACE

Until I was instructed in my first **sepsis** case several years ago, I had barely heard of it. I imagine that outside the medical community, apart from those who have been unfortunate enough to have experienced it (or to know someone else who has), that such ignorance is common. The newspapers report cases of death from sepsis, without explaining what it is, or else misdescribe it as 'blood poisoning'.

Part of my intention in writing this book is to provide a brief reference guide for lawyers and others involved in medico-legal work which explains in simple language what this condition is, how it comes about, and how it can (or ought to be) treated.

This book is necessarily highly medical. The law for claims involving sepsis and **meningitis** is, in essence, no different from the law in any other area of clinical negligence. What sets sepsis and meningitis (and meningococcal disease) claims apart is the infectious diseases medical background, the high incidence of children and young people affected, and the almost invariably catastrophic consequences for the patient.

Sepsis is a devastating complication, and is the most common cause of hospital death both in this country and worldwide. It deserves to be better understood. Further, lawyers who understand it better will be better advisors and advocates.

Meningitis is better known, probably because awareness in the medical profession of sepsis has been slow. Further, due to its terrifying consequences, it is something that every doctor should seek to rule out in any acute presentation, particularly in children. Everyone knows about the textbook symptoms of '**meningism**': a stiff neck, **photophobia** and headache. However, these symptoms do not usually present in young children, which is the highest risk group for meningitis.

It was not until after I had completed the first draft of this book that I had my own personal experience of meningitis. My son, at four days old developed enterovirus meningitis. Fortunately, we took him to hospital promptly, where he received excellent care, and he went on to make a good recovery. Sadly, not everyone will have the same experience when meningitis strikes, either in terms of the level of care received, or the ultimate outcome.

This book will set out the signs and symptoms that commonly occur, with the hope that in a claim that has not yet been litigated and where expert evidence has not yet been obtained, a lawyer will know what to look for in the medical notes, and what questions to ask the claimant or the claimant's family, and any expert who is later instructed.

There has been an increase in recent years in cases involving both sepsis and meningitis. These cases almost always involve difficult questions on causation, although breach of duty is not always straightforward either.

My aim is to explore the medicine is some detail before turning to the issues that will arise in litigation. I will explore some of the decisions in the area, and attempt to offer simple and practical advice on how to avoid some of the pitfalls that arise.

This book is written mainly with a claimant audience in mind, which reflects my own clinical negligence practice. It is also presumed that defendants (litigants, if not their solicitors) come to the table with a higher degree of background knowledge in the medicine.

I make the point that although much of this book will be concerned with providing medical explanations, I am not medically qualified. I am, however, married to a doctor to whom I owe a debt of gratitude in helping me to understand and explain some relatively complex medicine in what I hope is simple and intelligible language. I am also hugely indebted to Dr Nelly Ninis who provided me with considerable assistance on the medicine.

There is a glossary at the end of this book. Any medical term which appears in bold on first use is defined within it.

All the law quoted within this book is believed to be accurate as at 5 September 2019.

Isaac Hogarth
12 King's Bench Walk
September 2019

# ACKNOWLEDGEMENTS

I would like to express my immense gratitude to Dr Nelly Ninis for her expert and detailed review of the medical chapters of this book and for her invaluable input, which has been extensive. I thank her for being so generous with her time.

Thanks to the team at Law Brief Publishing, and in particular to Tim Kevan for approaching me to write this book.

Thanks to my colleagues at 12 King's Bench Walk, and in particular my senior colleagues, who are always available to help, in particular: William Audland QC, Stephen Worthington QC, Patrick Vincent, Richard Viney, David Sanderson and Henry Charles.

Thanks to my parents, Lydia and David, and to my wife, Raya.

# TABLE OF CASES

# TABLE OF LEGISLATION

## Primary Legislation



## Statutory Instruments

# CONTENTS

# CHAPTER ONE
# INTRODUCTION

Sepsis and meningitis are separate and distinct conditions (although they may present together) and in many ways, each deserves its own book. However, in a medico-legal context, the claims in which these conditions arise, are likely to have much in common. The facts will invariably concern time-critical medical emergencies arising from infection and the consequences of infection, where the outcome is likely to be catastrophic injury or death. There is a significant degree of cross-over in terms of the expert evidence that would be required.

The following disciplines are commonly instructed to consider breach of duty:

- General practitioners: where there has been a GP attendance or telephone consultation and either no referral, or a delayed referral

- Emergency medicine doctors: where there has been an attendance at A&E but where the signs and symptoms have not been properly recognised or there has been a delay in initiating life-saving treatment

- General paediatricians: who (in cases involving children) will typically take over after the Emergency Department (ED) and before Paediatric Intensive Care (PICU)

- Intensive care (ICU) doctors: in cases where there is a question as to whether the patient was appropriately managed during a period of ICU admission

- Surgeons: where a wound has become infected post-operatively and there is a failure to recognise the severity such that sepsis is allowed to develop, or failure to recognise intra-abdominal sepsis (e.g. arising from acute appendicitis)

The following disciplines are commonly instructed to consider causation:

- Experts in infectious diseases: to report on what treatment would have been given had an infectious diseases opinion been sought (although this may be provided by an acute general physician or emergency doctor, depending on the factual background) and on the natural history of the condition and what treatments may or may not have changed the outcome

- Microbiologists: to report on the development of the condition, and what the likely effect of certain treatments would have been had they been started earlier. As will be seen from the recent decisions in the High Court in meningitis and meningococcal disease claims, the Court will often work backwards with the help of the microbiologists in constructing a hypothetical timeline for how the disease is likely to have been developing. It is on this basis that causation will often be decided

- Neurologists: to report on the cause and extent of any brain damage and timing of events such as stroke or the development of hydrocephalus (a condition in which **cerebrospinal fluid** (CSF) builds up which can be caused by meningitis)

- Neuroradiologists: to report on the exact nature of brain injury

The medicine and the medical language are not straightforward.

This book will attempt to explain a little of the aetiology behind these conditions, and explore the signs and symptoms that a diagnosing primary or secondary care doctor ought to be looking for. Medical terms are defined in context as they appear, but there is also a glossary as the end of the book.

Whilst there has long been an awareness of meningitis and meningococcal disease, awareness of sepsis (including within the medical profession) has significantly improved within the past few years. This is most obviously demonstrated by the introduction of a new Guideline published by the National Institute for Health and Care Excellence (NICE) in July 2016,[1] and a resolution by the World Health Organisation (WHO) Seventieth World Health Assembly in May 2017.[2]

Claims arising from sepsis are not entirely new (a claim arising from puerperal sepsis reached the House of Lords in 1936,[3] albeit this was a case about infection control, rather than negligent treatment). It is also worth noting that various of the early cases which refer to 'sepsis', use that word as a synonym for 'infection'.[4] That is not the manner in which it is now used, which is explained in detail below.

It is interesting to note that there were six reported cases in 2018, eight in 2017 and eight in 2016, and this is against the fact that very few matters arising from clinical negligence come to trial. Whilst it is therefore impossible to estimate how many claims involving sepsis there are, considering (i) the rise in reported cases (ii) the general rise in recorded instances within the NHS, (iii) the publication of treatment standards against which to benchmark care, and (iv) that due to the speed with which sepsis develops and the need for urgent intervention, it is the sort of condition in which negligence may occur with serious consequences, it is safe to presume that the number of cases is very significant.

---

1 https://www.nice.org.uk/guidance/ng51/resources

2 http://apps.who.int/gb/ebwha/pdf_files/WHA70/A70_R7-en.pdf?ua=1&ua=1

3 *Lindsey CC v Marshall* [1937] AC 97.

4 As in *Mahon v Osborne* [1939] 2 KB 14, which is a case in which a surgeon had left a surgical swab inside the plaintiff's abdomen at the end of s surgical procedure. The Court talked of the "obvious danger of sepsis" from the plaintiff's stomach contents, which had escaped into a cavity in the duodenum due to the presence of an ulcer. Likewise, in *Roe v Minister of Health* [1954] 2 QB 66 at 76.

There are fewer cases involving meningitis or meningococcal disease, and very few reported cases. This is because it is significantly rarer than sepsis, but also because the vast majority of such claims will settle. The most recent reported first instance decision in a meningitis claim was in 2016.[5]

In order to understand sepsis, meningitis and meningococcal disease, it is first necessary to have a basic understanding of infection and how it works, which is dealt with in the following chapter.

5 *XYZ (A Child) v Maidstone v Tunbridge Wells NHS Trust* [2016] EWHC 2687 (QB). See further below at p.75.

# CHAPTER TWO
# AN OVERVIEW OF INFECTION

To understand sepsis, it is necessary first to understand the basic pathophysiology of infection.

Infection is a disorder caused by the invasion of pathogenic (i.e. causing of disease) microorganisms in the body. These are generally viral or bacterial but can also be fungal or parasitic.

Many bacteria (pathogenic or otherwise) co-exist on the human body without causing infection or any symptoms. For instance, one in 10 adults will carry a **meningococcus** in the oropharynx at any stage and young children are frequently colonised with a number of pneumococci in their upper airway. Invasive disease will only occur if these organisms gain access to the internal body and a usually sterile site such as the blood or cerebrospinal fluid (CSF).

Acquisition of these organisms is usually from other humans.

The pathogens will enter the body and become invasive either because of a breach in the body's defences or decreased immunity or because a pathogen with high virulence is acquired. Other portals of entry can include contaminated food or water, cuts, surgery (especially when plastic or metal devices are placed in the body such as a shunt or a pin/plate).

Bacteria and viruses are pathologically different, and usually work in very different ways.

## Bacteria

Bacteria are self-sufficient single-celled organisms. Most carry a single molecule of DNA. Bacteria reproduce by binary fission, whereby the cell will divide into two. Bacteria are divided up into gram-negative and gram-positive. Common pathogenic bacteria include:

Gram-negative:

- E-coli (Escherichia coli). This is a bacterium that lives in the gut of healthy people. Several strains are contained in undercooked meat or contaminated water, and can cause diarrhoea, and in rare cases, kidney failure. E.coli is a cause of very serious early onset neonatal infection

- Meningococcus (Neisseria meningitidis). It is thought that around 10% of the population carry the meningococcus bacterium in the nasopharynx at any given time. This bacterium can (as described below) result in meningococcal disease and meningitis

Gram-positive:

- **Pneumococcus** (Streptococcus pneumoniae). This bacterium is carried in the nasopharynx of a large portion of the population, especially children and young people. It is the main cause of community acquired pneumonia and meningitis in children and the elderly. It can also cause **pneumococcal** infections other than pneumonia, and sepsis

- Staphylococcus. Staphyloccoci colonise on the skin and mucous membranes, and mostly cause skin infections, although they can cause more serious infections including **bacteraemia**, **sepsis**, and **toxic shock syndrome**

- Streptococcus. There are many species of streptococcus. Group A strep are found on the surface of the skin and inside the throat, and can cause a range of infections including pneumonia, meningitis, as well as less serious infections like tonsillitis, cellulitis and sinusitis

Tuberculosis (can appear either gram-positive or -negative):

- Mycobacterium tuberculosis. This can cause tuberculosis (TB), which is an infection generally affecting the lungs, although TB can affect other parts of the body. A quarter of the world's population is thought to be infected, although only 10% of latent infections progress to active disease. In rare cases, this bacterium can infect the **meninges**, causing TB meningitis. These cases are hard to diagnose before they have caused devastating brain injury, and are increasing in the UK

Any bacterium ending -coccus is formed of spheres. Streptococcus is a linear chain of spheres, and staphylococcus is a linear web of spheres. Neisseria species appear bean-shaped under the microscope.

Once bacteria have invaded the body (for instance, due to impaired immunity or high virulence of the pathogen), they start to multiply and generally release some form of toxin into the circulation in very high numbers. The immune system attacks the bacteria in a myriad of ways resulting in a 'cytokine storm' and initiating significant inflammation within the body. In essence, once white cells have detected the bacteria, and started to attack, the body increases blood flow in order to transport further appropriate cells to the nidus of infection, either in order to attack the bacteria, or to repair damaged cells. The capillaries will expand, and white cells called **phagocytes** will exit the blood vessels to engulf and destroy the bacteria.

A more detailed overview of infection in the context of sepsis and meningitis appears below.

**Viruses**

A virus is a very small pocket of protein containing genetic material (either RNA or DNA). Viruses are much smaller in size than bacteria (the polio virus is 50 times smaller than a streptococcus bacterium). Common viral illnesses include the common cold, influenza, gastroenteritis, glandular fever (caused by the Epstein Barr virus), measles, mumps, rubella, chickenpox/shingles, tonsillitis, HIV/AIDS, hepatitis, herpes, Ebola, polio and viral meningitis (usually caused by enterovirus, mumps or herpes simplex).[1]

Viruses are either polyhedral (usually 20-sided), spherical, helical (rod-shaped) or complex.

Once a virus enters a host cell, it takes over the metabolic functions (i.e. biochemical reactions and processes at cellular level) of the host and causes it to reproduce more of the virus. This triggers an immune response through the release by the host cells of **interferons**, a group of signalling proteins (a type of **cytokine**). Interferons do not fight the virus directly, but prompt surrounding cells to produce proteins that prevent the virus from replicating within them. Interferons also assist white cells in fighting infection through signalling and regulation. One of the effects of the release of cytokines is inflammation.

### Inflammation

Inflammation is part of the body's response to infection.

There are four normal signs of inflammation (when it is visible, for example a skin or bone/joint infection): swelling, redness (or '**erythema**'), heat, and pain. These signs are the consequences of an increase in blood flow and capillary permeability (i.e. the ability of the blood vessel wall to become permeable to allow for the flow of small molecules), the increased presence of white cells (phagocytes in particular), and tissue damage.

Considering those matters in turn:

- The increase in blood flow is caused by constriction of the capillaries that carry blood from the infected area, which then leads to engorgement (distention with fluid) of the capillaries at the site of infection

1 On which see further p.21.

- Erythema occurs naturally in response to the build-up of blood in an area of the body due to engorgement of the capillary network and the release of histamine, a mediator of inflammation

- Increased capillary permeability can lead to fluid build-up as water and plasma proteins leak out of vessels into the tissues

**Systemic inflammatory response syndrome (SIRS)**

Inflammation throughout the body occurs when bacteria are invasive and an immune response is triggered. This inflammation will cause symptoms in the patient. (The term SIRS has been abandoned in terms of defining if a patient is septic, but it is very useful to understand how the body responds to invading bacteria and how sepsis develops).

This is a serious inflammatory condition, which may be caused by bacterial infection (although there are also other causes). It is a consequence of activation of the immune system and the consequent 'cytokine storm' that results. SIRS is identified by the occurrence of two or more of the following clinical features:

- Temperature, instability, fever or **hypothermia**

- **Tachycardia**

- Reduced peripheral **perfusion** / prolonged capillary refill time

- Altered mental state (floppiness / irritability / lethargy / sleeping in children)

- **Leucocytosis** (an increase in white blood cells) or **leucopoenia** (a reduction in the number of white blood cells).

In cases of severe infection, the inflammatory response can lead to sepsis and **septic shock**.

### Fever

The body will normally also develop a temperature in response to an infection. This helps fight infection in two ways. Firstly, it slows the rate of bacteria growth. Secondly, a raised temperature is actually thought to stimulate the immune response.[2] The fever can be generated both by the pathogen itself (for instance, there are cell-wall components of types of bacteria which can generate fever), and by cytokines (this is part of SIRS).

### Resisting infection

Inflammation and fever are only a part of a complex set of structures and processes that activate in order to fight infection. A full explanation of the workings of the immune system is beyond the scope of this book.

In the cases of most infections, the body's own defences will generally be effective in fighting the pathogen, without any adverse or catastrophic outcome. In cases of bacterial infection, antibiotics will assist, by either killing, or inhibiting the growth of bacteria. There are, however, cases where serious bacterial infection will not resolve without the help of proper and swift administration of appropriate antibiotic therapy.

---

2 Evans, Sharon S, Repasky, Elizabeth A, Fisher, Daniel T, 'Fever and the thermal regulation of immunity: the immune system feels the heat' Nat Rev Immunol. 2015 Jun; 15(6): 335–349.

# CHAPTER THREE
# SEPSIS

## What is sepsis?

Unlike an infection like meningitis or pneumonia, sepsis is not a stand-alone illness or disease. It is rather the body's overactive inflammatory response to severe infection and is a medical emergency, which can lead to tissue damage, multi-**organ failure**, and death. It is not the same thing as septicaemia,[1] which is blood poisoning caused by large numbers of bacteria in the bloodstream, although the two are often conflated or confused with one another (as **septicaemia** will lead to a state of sepsis). As of 2016, the technical internationally recognised definition is "life-threatening organ dysfunction caused by a dysregulated host response to infection."[2]

As described above, when there is a significant bacterial infection, the immune response causes systemic inflammation (SIRS). This inflammation will damage the lining of all the vessels in the body causing them to become leaky. Water and proteins from the blood will leak into the tissues of the body and reduce the circulating blood volume. The pumping of the heart is also affected by toxins produced by the bacteria. The body will compensate for reduced blood volume by making the heart pump faster to maintain the blood pressure. Blood is diverted away from the peripheries (hands and feet) and the kidneys. The aim of this 'cardiac compensation' is to maintain perfusion of the heart and brain as long as possible. The coagulation system is deranged making the blood less coagulable and the platelets also fall. A state of **septic shock** occurs when the circulation is inadequate to meet the body's needs.

---

1 On which see further p.30.

2 Singer M, Deutschman CS, Seymour CW et al, The Third International Consensus Definitions for Sepsis and Septic Shock (Sepsis-3), *JAMA* 2016;315:801-810

When sepsis is severe, the blood pressure may drop due to loss of fluid from the circulating volume. Organ failure may then arise from decreased flow of blood and oxygen. Septic shock in adults is characterised by low blood pressure despite adequate fluid replacement, and organ dysfunction or failure. In children, septic shock usually occurs with a normal blood pressure, and a fall in blood pressure is a late and very ominous sign.

The diagnosis of sepsis is clinical (i.e. a diagnosis made on the basis of signs and symptoms rather than diagnostic tests) with a few simple laboratory tests such as lactate.

However, there is new and ongoing research into developing a laboratory diagnosis. A very recent paper published in February 2019,[3] and widely reported in the national press,[4] published the details of research into a test which measures a protein biomarker of sepsis (interleukin-6, which is a cytokine), using a microelectrode integrated into a needle shaped substrate, which it is claimed could provide results within two-and-a-half minutes. It will be interesting to see how this research develops, and whether this device becomes a part of NHS care.

The NICE Guideline has a stated aim of raising awareness within the medical profession such that when a patient presents with infection, the treating professional should ask themselves the question 'could this be sepsis?'.

## Septic shock

Septic shock in adults is defined as persisting **hypotension** requiring **vasopressors** (medicines that cause blood vessels to contract and raise blood pressure) to maintain a mean arterial pressure of 65mmHg or

---

3 Russell, Christopher; Ward, Andrew C; Vezza, Vincent; Hoskisson, Paul; Alcorn, David; Steenson, D Paul; Corrigan, Damion K, Development of a needle shaped microelectrode for electrochemical detection of the sepsis biomarker interleukin-6 (IL-6) in real time, *Biosensors & bioelectronics*, 126 (2019), 806-814

4 https://www.bbc.co.uk/news/health-47279072

more and having a serum lactate (a marker detected in a blood gas, which becomes raised when a patient is severely septic) level of greater than 2 mmol/l despite adequate volume resuscitation.

In essence that means a low blood pressure and a raised lactate level, not improving with intravenous fluids.

Clinical features of septic shock are:

- Fever with severe shaking (rigors)
- Muscle aches and severe discomfort
- Dizziness
- Fast pulse rate (tachycardia)
- Shortness of breath / fast breathing/ **tachypnoea**
- Cold or mottled skin
- Poor urine output
- Low blood pressure
- Confusion

Treatment will normally require ICU admission with fluids, intravenous antibiotics, vasopressors, and respiratory support.

Septic shock in children differs in that hypotension is not required to make the diagnosis. The particulars of paediatric septic shock are covered in Chapter 4 under the section on meningococcal sepsis.

Loss of peripheral tissues through gangrene can develop in some infections (particularly meningococcal infection or group A streptococcal sepsis) as a result of lack of blood flow and disturbance of the coagulation system. This is known as **purpura fulminans**.

If a bacterial infection originating in gangrenous tissue spreads, that can cause septic shock.

## Spotting sepsis

There are several risk factors for developing sepsis, which any doctor should be aware of. These are not new within the NHS. Even before the new Sepsis Guideline was published in July 2016, these factors were taught as part of compulsory life support and paediatric life support training.[5]

However, since that Guideline was published, any doctor in a primary (i.e. GP) or secondary care (i.e. hospital) setting ought to be acutely aware of the relevant factors, and at the very least, ought to have the Guideline in mind (and use it as a point of reference) when assessing an acutely ill patient.

The following groups are at higher risk of developing sepsis:[6]

- The very young and the very old (i.e. under 1 or over 75), or the very frail
- Those with impaired immune systems due to illness (e.g. those with diabetes) or medications (e.g. whilst undergoing chemo-therapy)
- Anyone who has undergone a recent surgery, or other invasive procedure
- People with cuts, burns, blisters or skin infections
- Intravenous drug users
- People with indwelling lines or catheters

---

5 ALS and APLS course materials, published by the Advanced Life Support Group

6 Paragraph 1.2 of the Sepsis Guideline

- Women who have recently given birth, had a termination of pregnancy or miscarriage in the previous six weeks

The Guideline is very helpful in that it sets out algorithms in both written and tabular form for different age groups, and differentiates between patients in a hospital setting and those outside a hospital setting.

The following are high risk warning signs that apply generally, albeit that each factor is generally dependent on the age of the patient:[7]

(a) **History:**

- ○ Objective evidence of altered behaviour or mental state
- ○ Appears ill to a healthcare professional (particularly in children)
- ○ Does not wake, or if roused, does not stay awake

(b) **Respiratory:**

- ○ Raised respiratory rate or tachypnoea (e.g. for a person over 12 years a respiratory rate (RR) of more than 25 breaths per minute, for a child aged 5 an RR of more than 29, for a child aged 1 to 2 an RR of more than 50)
- ○ Decreased oxygen saturations (generally less than 90% in air)

(c) **Circulation and hydration**

- ○ Low heartrate or **bradycardia** (a heartrate of less than 60 beats per minute (bpm) in a child of 11 or under)

7 Please note the following is not the full guideline, but rather a series of examples taken from it. The full guideline is available at https://www.nice.org.uk /guidance/ng51/resources

- Rapid heartrate tachycardia (for a person aged 12 years or more 130 beats per minute (bpm), for a child aged 6-7 years 120 bpm or more, for a baby under 1 a heartrate of 160 bpm or more))

(d) Skin

- Mottled (irregular appearance caused by blood vessel changes) or ashen appearance (skin looking grey or pale, due to lack of oxygenation)

- **Cyanosis** of skin, lips or tongue (bluish discolouration, also caused by **hypoxia**, or lack of oxygenation)

- Non-blanching rash (i.e. a skin rash that does not fade under pressure)

Perhaps surprisingly, body temperature is not a high-risk factor except:

(a) in children under 5 years, in which case a temperature of less than 36°C is a high-risk factor

(b) in children under 3 months in which case a temperature of over 38°C is a high-risk factor.

**Treatment**

According to the Guideline all people with suspected sepsis outside an acute hospital setting should be referred for emergency medical care by the most appropriate means of transport if they meet any of the above high-risk criteria.

The treatment the patient would then receive in a hospital setting depends on their age.

For example, for a child aged 5-11, with any high-risk criteria (or with two or more moderate to high risk criteria under the Guideline), the protocol is:

- to arrange for immediate review by the senior clinical decision maker to assess the child and think about alternative diagnoses to sepsis
- to carry out a venous blood test
- to give broad spectrum antibiotics (what antibiotic is to be given will often depend on local trust-based protocols or guidelines)
- discuss with a consultant (noting that if the admission takes place at night, for instance, the most senior paediatrician in the hospital is likely to be a registrar)
- where lactate is raised, give an intravenous fluid bolus (a means of rapid rehydration)

While sepsis is suspected (and indeed for any patient in a hospital setting undergoing treatment for acute infection), monitoring should be in place at least every 30 minutes.

Tools like the national early warning score (NEWS) or paediatric early warning score (PEWS) should be in place, and will be an indication after the event of how ill the patient was considered to be. However, these tools are not always consistently applied, such that there is limited weight that can be attached to these scores.

**Outcomes**

Many people who suffer sepsis, including those who become critically ill, make a full recovery. The extent of recovery, and how long it takes, will usually depend on the severity of the sepsis, the overall state of the patient's health, the duration of hospital admission, and whether the patient required treatment in an intensive care unit.

Many of the cases that involve sepsis will be fatal cases. Precise statistics about the number of deaths from sepsis are hard to come by, as, because sepsis will arise in the context of an underlying illness or infection, it is not always recorded. The Office of National Statistics (ONS) mortality data for 2017 records only 2,705 deaths as being from sepsis. Based on research, and other data, that figure is probably a gross under-reflection of the true number.

One paper,[8] published following a systematic review of 15 international citation databases for population-level estimates of sepsis incidence and fatality data, gave figures of hospital mortality of 17% for sepsis and 26% for severe sepsis in the period 2005 to 2015.

The Sepsis Trust estimates that 52,000 people in the UK die every year from sepsis. In August 2018, the BBC reported that following an analysis of NHS mortality data at 133 NHS trusts, recorded deaths from sepsis had increased by 38% between April 2015 and April 2017.[9]

In a 2016 paper,[10] it was said that in the first year following an episode of sepsis, 60% of patients will have at least one rehospitalisation episode, and at least one in six will die. Survivors also have a higher risk of cognitive impairment and cardiovascular disease, resulting in a reduced life expectation.

In an American study of patients of over 65 years admitted to hospital with sepsis, it was suggested that mortality following the episode may be

8 Fleischmann C, Scherag A, Adhikari NK, Hartog CS, Tsaganos T, Schlattmann P et al. 'Assessment of Global Incidence and Mortality of Hospital-treated Sepsis – Current Estimates and Limitations.' *Am J Respir Crit Care Med.* 2015. doi:10.1164/rccm.201504-0781OC

9 https://www.bbc.co.uk/news/health-45045438. It should be noted that NHS England responded that the statistics were unreliable as previous cases of sepsis had not been properly categorised

10 Shankar-Hari M, Rubenfeld GD. 'Understanding Long-Term Outcomes Following Sepsis: Implications and Challenges.' *Curr Infect Dis Rep.* 2016;18:37. doi: 10.1007/s11908-016-0544-7

as high as one in five, and that the mortality remained higher for at least two years relative to adults not in hospital.[11]

Due to the increased risk of readmission and death, if following a septic episode, there is readmission or death, even where it is not immediately apparent that such was caused by the septic episode, a claimant will need to ask their experts to comment on causation (which may involve a literature review).

Some patients will experience lethargy, muscle weakness, rheumatic swelling and pain, chest pain or breathlessness, which may fall within what is described as 'Post Sepsis Syndrome' (PSS). Relatively little has been written on this diagnosis, although the NHS webpage on sepsis[12] now recognises the possibility of a patient developing PSS, and links to the Sepsis Trust's information page on the subject.[13] There is not a single reported case (including quantum report on Lawtel) which refers to this diagnosis. This may be because the diagnosis is relatively new. I could locate only one paper (from June 2018)[14] which examined the diagnosis.

It is likely that PSS will become a more common feature in litigation. This is because the sort of symptoms which can be attributed to it may have been diagnosed as separate conditions not directly linked to the sepsis. For example, in the case of *Welsh v Walsall Healthcare NHS Trust* [2018] EWHC 1917 (QB), the claimant, who had suffered from sepsis following negligent management after a bowel perforation during

11 Prescott HC, Osterholzer JJ, Langa KM, Angus DC, Iwashyna TJ. 'Late mortality after sepsis: propensity matched cohort study.' *BMJ.* 2016;353. doi:10.1136/bmj.i2375

12 https://www.nhs.uk/conditions/sepsis/

13 https://sepsistrust.org/get-support/support-for-survivors/post-sepsis-syndrome/

14 Huang CY, Daniels R, Lembo A, Hartog C, O'Brien J, Heymann T, Reinhart K, Nguyen HB, 'Sepsis Survivors Engagement Project (SSEP); Life after sepsis: an international survey of survivors to understand the post-sepsis syndrome,' International Journal for Quality in Health Care, mzy137, https://doi.org/10.1093/intqhc/mzy137

surgery, went on to be diagnosed with fibromyalgia and chronic pain. In a post-septic patient, it is suggested that a diagnosis of PSS could probably be made in the alternative.

# CHAPTER FOUR
# MENINGITIS AND MENINGOCOCCAL DISEASE

**What are meningitis and meningococcal disease?**

Meningitis is an infection of the meninges, which are membranes that surround the brain and spinal cord. There are several types of meningitis, although **bacterial meningitis** is the type that is most likely to arise in a litigation background.

Meningococcal disease is any infection caused by the bacterium Neisseria meningitidis. This can include meningitis, septicaemia or a mixed presentation of meningitis with sepsis.

By far the most common type of meningitis is viral. Several viruses may cause meningitis, although the most common are enteroviruses. Unlike bacterial meningitis, viral meningitis is not considered to be contagious. It is also very rarely life-threatening (with the exception of herpes simplex meningoencephalitis). Further, there is generally no treatment, although patients need to be kept well-hydrated.

The most common bacterial pathogens which cause meningitis in the UK are the meningococcus, streptococcus and TB. Other bacteria which may cause meningitis include haemophilus and group A streptococcus.

In neonates (children younger than 28 days) and infants up to three months of life, meningitis may be caused by pathogens such as group B streptococcus. Early onset sepsis/meningitis occurs in the first week of life, caused by gram-negative bacteria (such as E.coli) and Group B streptococcus. Listeria occasionally causes meningitis in infants under eight weeks of age. Rather than originating in the upper respiratory tract (as with other patients who develop pneumococcal or meningococcal meningitis), these pathogens are found in the mother's gut or genital tract and are introduced through exposure during childbirth.

Meningitis develops in the following stages:

1. Exposure to the pathogen. In the case of pneumococcus or meningococcus, this is found in the flora of the upper respiratory tract.

2. Colonisation of the naso-orophyrangeal mucosa.

3. Passage through the mucosa.

4. Survival of the bacteria in the bloodstream. Once a high enough level of bacteraemia is reached, the **blood-brain barrier** is breached.

5. Inoculation of the cerebrospinal fluid by the bacteria which crossed the blood brain barrier.

6. Replication of the bacteria in the CSF and development of an inflammatory response.

7. Development of frank meningitis with clinical symptoms.

The description within the judgment of HHJ Oliver-Jones QC in *Coakley v Rosie* [2014] EWHC 1790 (QB) in the context of meningococcal meningitis is detailed and very helpful, and quotes from several authoritative papers:

> *8 When bacteria enter the bloodstream they can survive and proliferate by virtue of particular bacterial virulence factors or incompleteness of the host defence. Importantly, the proliferation of bacteria is exponential with a doubling of numbers, and thus bacterial 'load' or 'biomass', about every 45 minutes. This exponential growth is... and is of particular importance to the issue of causation viz. whether earlier antibiotic treatment would have prevented or materially reduced injury. Once viable meningococci have reached the bloodstream, known as bacteraemia, different disease manifesta-*

*tions can develop. Where there are low degrees of bacteraemia, meningococci are cleared spontaneously by the individual's immune system (the 'host immune response'), leaving behind a so-called transient meningococcaemia, characterised by a short febrile flu-like episode. Where the bacteraemia is not cleared, clinically overt disease develops; one such is meningococcal septic shock, another is meningitis:*

> *"In nearly all patients who develop* ***shock*** *and in most patients with meningitis, the beginning of the bacteraemic phase is marked by the onset of chills, acute fever, low back pain, thigh pain or generalised muscle aches. Within a few hours 'fulminant meningococcal sepsis' (FMS) may develop without signs of meningitis. This condition is characterised by high concentrations of* ***endotoxin*** *and cytokines in plasma. Because one of the striking features of meningococci is their propensity to invade the meninges, patients with less marked bacterial proliferation in the bloodstream and less* ***cytokinaemia****, present after 18 to 36 hours with meningitis. In these patients…blood cultures are often negative at the time of hospitalisation. Due to the limited growth of bacteria in the bloodstream and the seeding of meningococci in the subarachnoid space, patients with meningitis have compartmentalised high concentrations of endotoxin and cytokines in the CSF."*[1]

*9 Once meningococci cross the Blood-Brain Barrier and enter the CSF, then, without antibiotics, they are initially able to proliferate uncontrolled, because the host defence mechanisms, principally immunoglobulin and complement, are absent in the CSF. Consequently:*

> *"…the CSF can be conceptualised as a localised area of host immunodeficiency facilitating unrestrained proliferation of*

1 Quoting from 'Update on Meningococcal Disease with Emphasis on Pathogenesis and Clinical Management: Marcel Van Dueren and Others, Clin Microbiol Rev 2000;13:144-66

> *(the pathogen) which, if untreated, overwhelms the host until death."*[2]

*and*

> *"The inflammatory processes, including cytokine appearance, which cause tissue injury, begin within a few hours of the arrival of bacteria in the CSF ... In meningococcal infections, endotoxin is shed liberally from the surface of the meningococci by a process of blebbing [protrusions of the cell membrane, and a feature of cell physiology during cell movement]. There is a significant correlation between fatality rate and the quantity of endotoxin in the blood on presentation, and such bacterial components cause inflammation by inducing formation of host-derived cytokines ...*[3]

*Although the cytokines regulate the attack on the pathogen, the cellular damage to the host which they also cause, will itself initiate a further cytokine response. Hence what is called 'the cytokine cascade'..."*

To explain some of the above content:

- Blood-brain barrier (BBB) is the name of the semipermeable membrane that separates circulating blood from the brain and cerebrospinal fluid (CSF). Whilst water, glucose and amino acids can pass, the membrane is highly selective, and generally efficient at keeping bacteria out. However, when the meninges become inflamed the BBB may become disrupted, which can allow harmful substances to breach the barrier.

---

2 Quoting from Koedel et al 'Pathogenesis and pathophysiology of pneumococcal meningitis' Lancet Infect Dis. 2002 Dec;2(12):721-36

3 Quoting from N Begg et al: 'Consensus Statement on Diagnosis, Investigation, Treatment and Prevention of Acute Bacterial Meningitis in Immunocompetent Adults' J Infect. 1999 Jul;39(1):1-15

- Cerebrospinal fluid (CSF) is the fluid that surrounds the brain and the spinal cord. In order to make a positive diagnosis of meningitis, a lumbar puncture is required in which a sample of CSF is taken. In a person with meningitis, the CSF shows a low glucose level, increased white cell count and increased protein levels. CSF analysis will also help to diagnose which bacterium is causing the disease.

- 'Fulminant Meningococcal Sepsis', which in England would normally be referred to as 'meningococcal septicaemia', occurs when bacteria enter the blood and multiply, releasing toxins and causing the blood vessels to become damaged, which can then lead to organ damage and septic shock.

To summarise the pathophysiology of meningococcal infection:

(a) The bacteria penetrate the defensive mucosal lining of the nose and throat to enter the bloodstream;

(b) Once in the bloodstream, meningococci double their numbers every 30 to 45 minutes;

(c) As the meningococci multiply, they shed blebs from their outer coat, which contain endotoxin;

(d) The presence of endotoxin causes white cells to engulf the bacteria, which leads to the release of pro-inflammatory cytokines, which damages the **endothelial lining** of blood vessels;

(e) Endothelial damage activates the **coagulation cascade**, leading to clotting disturbance. Blood and other fluid leaks from the damaged vessels into the surrounding tissue;

(f) In extreme cases, widespread clotting in peripheries or limbs can lead to tissue hypoxia and necrosis (i.e. cell death), which may result in amputation. Likewise, the process can lead to organ failure or death.

(g) In some cases, they cross the BBB, producing inflammation in the meninges, which may cause raised intracranial pressure, which can cause neurological damage and death (these patients do not usually also have severe septic shock).

It will be understood that the reaction at (e) to (g) involves sepsis (i.e. an auto-inflammatory response, as described in the previous chapter), albeit one that is caused by an infection in the bloodstream (septicaemia), which in turn, is caused by the presence of meningococci.

It is possible for patients to suffer meningitis without septicaemia, which can still cause brain damage and death, but would not present with a rash, or symptoms of shock.

It is also possible for patients to suffer meningococcal septicaemia without meningitis, and the literature suggests that these are the patients with the poorest prognosis.[4]

**Diagnosing meningitis**

Just as the 2016 Sepsis Guideline is important when considering how sepsis is diagnosed, there is a NICE guideline which deals with meningitis and septicaemia in children: 'Meningitis (bacterial) and meningococcal septicaemia in under 16s: recognition, diagnosis and management', which was published on 23 June 2010.

Bacterial meningitis or meningococcal septicaemia ought to be considered in the case of any presentation by a child or young person who is febrile, has vomiting or nausea, lethargy, is irritable or unsettled, has an ill appearance, is refusing food or drink, has a headache, has muscle aches/ joint pain, has respiratory symptoms or signs, or breathing difficulty.[5]

4 Stiehm, ER, Damrosch, D. Factors in the prognosis of meningococcal infection. Review of 63 cases with emphasis on recognition and management of the severely ill patient. *Journal of Paediatrics*. 1966;68(3)457-67.

5 As per Table 1, NICE Guideline, Meningitis (bacterial) and meningococcal septicaemia in under 16s: recognition, diagnosis and management.

Contrary to a common belief, however, the classical signs of meningitis (neck stiffness, bulging fontanelle, high-pitched cry) are often absent in infants and children below two years with bacterial meningitis.

The Guideline contains a table (Table 1) of signs and symptoms of bacterial meningitis and meningococcal septicaemia. The problem is that a lot of these signs are non-specific, such as fever, vomiting, headache, aches and pains, and refusing food and drink. These signs and symptoms may falsely reassure the examining professional that the illness is a straightforward infection.

The specific signs and symptoms the medical profession will be looking for are:

- Altered mental state: this is the absolute hallmark of meningitis and the exact clinical manifestations will be very age dependent
- In young children, irritability, drowsiness and/or significant lethargy
- Older children or young adults: confusion, combativeness, lethargy, fluctuating consciousness level
- Headache and vomiting are very common
- Bulging fontanelle in a baby
- Photophobia (i.e. sensitivity to light), although this is not seen in very young children
- Stiff neck, although this is not seen in very young children
- Coma, significantly depressed consciousness level or a fluctuating consciousness level

- **Paresis** (muscular weakness caused by nerve damage or disease). This is more typical of highly inflammatory pathogens such as TB and pneumococcus

- Signs of significantly raised intracranial pressure include reduced conscious level, falling pulse, rising blood pressure and pupil changes

In cases caused by the meningococcus, a classical non-blanching rash may be seen. It has a several forms:

- **Petechiae:** pinpoint non-blanching spots (although these are often also seen in viral illnesses)

- **Purpura:** larger non-blanching spots of greater than 2mm. This rash is always significant and does not occur in a viral infection. It will occur in patients with meningitis and features of sepsis

It should be borne in mind that rash may be less visible in darker skin tones. The medical professional should check the soles of the feet, the palms of hands, and the conjunctivae (the mucous membrane that covers the front of the eye and lines the insides of the eyelids).

The classic haemorrhagic rash of meningococcal disease can occur at any stage of the infection but is usually not an early sign. The underlying meningitis or septicaemia can be quite advanced before the rash emerges.

30% of petechial or purpuric rashes will start as blanching rashes and then progress.

A non-blanching rash is only seen in meningococcal infection, not in other bacterial causes of meningitis.

Some patients with meningitis will also have some signs of sepsis or **SIRS**. It is very unusual to have meningitis with significantly raised intracranial pressure and severe sepsis. Usually one process dominates the clinical picture, and this will dictate which management guideline is used. It is poorly understood why one patient will develop meningitis and another patient sepsis with the same organism.

History taking is extremely important. If a patient presents at a GP or in A&E, it is important to elicit the reason. The history taker should ask about the specific symptoms of septicaemia and meningitis.

A child or young person with an unexplained petechial rash and fever (or history of fever) should undergo bloodwork, including a full blood count, C-reactive protein (**CRP**) and blood gas (which measures the acid levels in the blood, which is a marker of serious infection).

The only way to obtain a laboratory diagnosis of bacterial meningitis is to perform a lumbar puncture (which is known as a 'spinal tap' in America). This involves a thin needle being inserted between the lower vertebrae, and a sample being taken of cerebrospinal fluid (CSF).

There are, however, several important contraindications to performing a lumbar puncture, including signs suggesting raised intracranial pressure (which can be caused by meningitis), shock, extensive or spreading purpura, and convulsions.

In fact, practitioners should be aware that inappropriate lumbar puncture where there is evidence of raised intracranial pressure may result in a brain injury and/or death.

A judgment on whether there is raised intracranial pressure should not require a CT scan to be performed and should be reached on the basis of clinical judgment.

Performing a lumbar puncture should not, however, delay the administration of **parenteral** antibiotics (i.e. other than oral: in some cases, it will not be possible to obtain venous access, or in other cases, a GP may want to administer an urgent dose of antibiotics while awaiting an ambulance. In these cases, the injection may be intramuscular rather than intravenous).

It is essentially the case that a child with a presentation typical of meningitis will be treated as having meningitis until proven otherwise.

## Meningococcal septicaemia

As described in the section above, sepsis can be caused by a variety of pathogens. Meningococcal septicaemia is particularly fulminant (severe and sudden) and can cause death from septic shock within hours of the first symptom. The UK has had a high incidence of meningococcal disease (MD) for many years, falling more recently in part due to new vaccination campaigns against the strains Men B, Men C and Men W.

The highest incidence of MD occurs in the first year of life when the fatality rate is also highest. Children under four years of age are at high risk and thereafter the incidence rates fall again until late adolescence when there is a second peak in incidence in the 15-19-year-old age group. Most cases of MD occur in previously completely well children.

The symptom development in children with MD is as follows:

- Initial non-specific symptoms of fever, vomiting, anorexia (not eating), headache. These symptoms last for about four hours in young children but up to eight hours in teenagers

- The first specific symptoms are those of sepsis, namely: leg pain, abnormal skin colour, cold hands and feet and thirst. In young children drowsiness and laboured breathing may occur

- The first classic symptom of MD is the rash which appears with a median time of eight hours after the first symptom in an infant, but as late as 16 hours in an older teenager. The rash may start as a blanching rash and then change to a haemorrhagic rash

- The symptoms of meningitis (bulging fontanelle, neck stiffness and photophobia) occur late if they occur at all. Many children will die of sepsis before any features of meningitis are seen. If they occur, they will be seen around 12-15 hours after disease onset. Coma, delirium and seizures will occur last

Shock is a clinical diagnosis, the signs of which are present due to circulatory failure. A child in early shock may be alert and have a normal blood pressure. Early signs of shock will include tachycardia, cool peripheries, pallor, decreased urine output and tachypnoea. As shock progresses, **metabolic acidosis**, hypoxia and increasing tachycardia and tachypnoea will be noted. Late signs of shock include drowsiness or agitation, and hypotension.

Meningococcal disease is not the only cause of a non-blanching rash, but a non-blanching rash should be presumed to be meningococcal disease unless shown otherwise. This is because one in 10 children with meningococcal disease dies, and most fatal cases occur within the first 24 hours of the onset of symptoms.

It should be borne in mind that by the time a rash is widespread or purpuric, the disease is probably at a very advanced stage, such that even aggressive treatment will not salvage the outcome.

## Treatment of meningitis

As with sepsis, there are very well-established management protocols for meningitis.

In children, the first treatment for bacterial meningitis (and sepsis) is intravenous antibiotics (usually ceftriaxone). Antibiotics should be administered within one hour of the recognition of sepsis or possible meningitis.

For children younger than three months the preferred antibiotics are cefotaxime plus either amoxicillin or ampicillin.

Treatment (both for children and adults) will be as follows:

1. Antibiotics – high dose, intravenous

2. Steroids to try to prevent deafness should be considered in patients older than 3 months

3. Recognise and manage raised intracranial pressure. If this occurs:

4. Admit to intensive care

    a. Treatments to decrease the pressure such as 3% saline / mannitol

    b. Intubation and ventilation with neuroprotection

    c. Brain imaging to recognise complications such as early hydrocephalus

5. Manage complications such as seizures

The matters to look at and consider in terms of the management are:

- Whether appropriate antibiotics were given in a timely manner (this should generally be done within a maximum of 60 minutes from the decision being made that they were needed)
- Whether there has been appropriate fluid management
- Have vital signs been monitored?
- Has the seriousness of the illness been appreciated?
- Has there been appropriate escalation?
- Has resuscitation been sufficiently aggressive?

For children and young people who suffer severe or profound deafness, they should be sent for urgent assessment for cochlear implants as soon as they are fit to do so.

Follow-up should otherwise include consideration of the following morbidities:

- Hearing loss
- Orthopaedic complications
- Skin complications (including scarring from necrosis)
- Psychosocial problems
- Neurological and developmental problems
- Renal failure.

**Outcomes**

Every year in the UK, there are between 1,000 and 2,000[6] cases of meningococcal disease, and around 5,000 to 6,000[7] cases of pneumococcal sepsis and meningitis.

Meningococcal disease is fatal in approximately 10% of cases. More deaths are caused by septicaemia (or rather, the resulting shock and/or multi-organ failure) than meningitis. About 20% of those who survive are left with serious long-term symptoms, including amputations, hearing loss and brain damage.

Around 15% of children with pneumococcal meningitis will die, and 25% will be left with severe, long-term effects, including hearing loss, sight loss, learning difficulties, or seizures.[8]

---

6 https://www.jenner.ac.uk/meningitis

7 http://vk.ovg.ox.ac.uk/pneumococcal-disease

8 http://vk.ovg.ox.ac.uk/pneumococcal-disease

# CHAPTER FIVE
# NON-EXPERT EVIDENCE

It will usually be the case when having to make a first review of prospects of a potential claim (including for the purposes of undertaking a risk assessment for the purposes of entering into a conditional fee agreement), that there is no expert evidence to assist the legal team in performing that review.

As in any clinical negligence case, there will be two main sources of evidence at this stage: (1) the client's account (or that of their family), and (2) the contemporaneous medical notes. In some cases, a client or their family will have made a complaint and received a reply.

## Serious Incident and Root Cause Analysis reports

In some cases, particularly those where a complaint has been made, the defendant (in the case of an NHS trust) may have undertaken a serious incident report. In accordance with guidance from NHS England, serious incidents (which are relevant for present purposes) include:

- unexpected or avoidable death
- unexpected or avoidable injury that has resulted in serious harm
- unexpected or avoidable injury that requires further treatment by a healthcare professional to prevent death or serious harm
- a 'never event'[1].

Alternatively, there may have been a more concise Root Cause Analysis (RCA) investigation. Trusts will typically have their own RCA template

1 As per the list of never events periodically published by NHS Improvement, the current edition of which may be found at: https://improvement.nhs.uk/documents/2899/Never_Events_list_2018_FINAL_v6.pdf

form, which will identify what happened and why, and consider the level of risk of recurrence. These reports tend to be significantly less detailed than full serious incident reports.

It should be noted that there is now a statutory 'duty of candour', which was introduced by way of The Health and Social Care Act 2008 (Regulated Activities) Regulations 2014 ('the 2014 Regulations'). For NHS trusts, a 'notifiable safety incident' under the 2014 Regulations is one that resulted in, or could have resulted in, the patient's death, or them suffering severe or moderate harm or prolonged psychological harm (reg.7).

As soon as reasonably practicable after becoming aware of a notifiable safety incident, a trust must notify the patient, and provide reasonable support.

Pursuant to regulation 20(3), the notification must:

(a) be given in person

(b) provide an account of all facts known about the incident

(c) advise what further enquiries the trust considers appropriate

(d) include an apology

(e) be recorded in a written record to be kept securely

It is to be noted that "apology" is defined as "an expression of sorrow or regret in respect of a notifiable safety incident. An apology does not necessarily mean that an admission of liability in a civil claim will be made, although if it is reasoned, and made in the context of obvious or admitted failings, it may be difficult for the defendant to escape liability.

NHS Resolution, its solicitors and counsel are well aware of, and frequently rely on, section 2 of the Compensation Act 2006, which provides:

> "*2. Apologies, offers of treatment or other redress*
>
> *An apology, an offer of treatment or other redress, shall not of itself amount to an admission of negligence or breach of statutory duty.*"

It may be argued that the authors of any report did not have the appropriate standard of care in mind when recording criticisms, i.e. they have had a higher standard in mind than would be applied by a court in reference to *Bolam v Friern Hospital Management Committee* [1957] 1 WLR 582 and *Bolitho v City and Hackney Health Authority* [1998] AC 232. If a denial of liability is received on that basis (in a case where there have been critical findings in a serious incident report), it would be a good idea to make an early request (in correspondence if pre-issue, or by way of Part 18 Request otherwise) for an explanation of what standard of duty the defendant says the author was applying in making such criticisms, and how that standard is different from *Bolam*. It would also be sensible to request disclosure of any documents relevant to the issue, including written instructions given to the authors of the incident report and any relevant policies or protocols.

It will occasionally happen that a defendant seeks to restrict, or limit the reliance which can be placed on, a serious incident report (or similar). It is sometimes suggested that such reliance is impermissible by virtue of the rule in *Hollington*:[2] that a judgment in prior proceedings is no evidence of the truth either of the decision or its grounds. Such a position is ill-conceived and wrong, in that the author of a serious incident report is not exercising a judicial or quasi-judicial function. The primary function of such a report is to investigate the facts in order to identify shortcomings in management such that a trust can learn from any errors that were made, and thereby avoid future repetition of such errors.

2 *Hollington v F Hewthorn & Co Ltd* [1943] KB 587

A serious incident report is plainly admissible, although its findings will (obviously) not bind a civil judge. The issue is analogous to the situation in *Rogers v Hoyle* [2014] EWCA Civ 257, a Court of Appeal decision on the admissibility of an independent, statutorily mandated report into an aviation accident. The defendant had sought to have the report excluded under the rule in *Hollington*, on the basis that the report was expert evidence but not compliant with Part 35 of the Civil Procedure Rules, or alternatively, under the Court's discretion to exclude such evidence under CPR r.32.1(2). The defendant's attempt failed at first instance and on appeal, the Court of Appeal holding that:

(a) The rule in *Hollington* was not engaged

(b) The report contained statements of fact and expressions of opinions of its authors, who were experts in their fields

(c) Any statements were hearsay, and admissible, subject to a discretion of the trial judge as to weight

(d) Part 35 did not engage as the report was not expert evidence prepared for the purposes of the proceedings

(e) As the report was admissible and of potential value, the circumstances in which the Court would exercise its discretion to exclude it under CPR r.32.1(2) were limited.

It is respectfully suggested that for the same reasons, a Court is most unlikely to restrict the admissibility of a serious incident report, albeit the Court is not bound by the findings of such a report (any more than it is bound by the expert evidence).

Witness evidence

In sepsis and meningitis cases, the timeline is of paramount importance. An account should be taken from the prospective claimant (and/or family members) which is as detailed as possible. Where matters are likely to be contentious, any other evidence which will corroborate the claimant's account should be investigated. This may include phone records and witness testimony from third parties.

The following facts and matters should be explored and recorded:

- Background and pre-existing health issues
- First onset of symptoms
- Details of initial symptoms and how they progressed
- First medical attendance, including full details of what information was relayed, whether anyone attended with the claimant, what advice was given, whether the doctor seemed concerned. Often a key matter will be whether the patient was instructed to return, and on what basis (i.e. if *x* symptoms developed, or if they were no better by *y* time).

There are certain details that sometimes stick in the mind of claimants (or their families), which may have had particular poignance to them, even if the medical professional did not think them important or did not record them. Such details can be key. For instance, if in a paediatric case against a GP, a parent specifically remembers having raised the fact that the child was breathing fast, or had a racing heartbeat, but this has not been recorded or measured in the notes, that may be good evidence that the GP did not take seriously important concerns that were raised.

As with all proofs of a witness, the questioner should ask open, non-leading questions, which provide the witness with an opportunity to tell the story. They should not be prompted or led to give an account if they are unable to remember details or facts. Open questions generally involve the words "what", "where", "when", "who", and "how". Likewise, unless there is an issue as to capacity or particular vulnerability, partners or other family members should not be allowed to interrupt and tell the story.

When dealing with older teenagers who have mental capacity, the same rule would apply, and parents should be asked to let them speak for themselves. With other children, in those cases where it is appropriate to take a statement, there is more of a balance to be struck, and parents will probably have to assist, albeit they should be advised in advance of the need to facilitate the child in giving their account, rather than doing all the work for them.

## The medical notes

There is no rule of law which says that medical notes are to be deemed more accurate than any other evidence. There are two important cases which explain the relevant principles.

The first, *W v Johnson* [2015] EWHC 276 (QB) is a case brought against a GP in relation to an alleged failure to refer a four-year-old boy who developed pneumococcal meningitis. There was a factual dispute between the claimant's parents and the defendant as to what symptoms were present at the time of a consultation. The claimant's parents alleged that W was at the time suffering from vomiting, headache and fever, which would have mandated immediate referral. The contemporaneous note made by the defendant recorded a temperature of 39.4°C, the absence of a rash, and nothing else of note.

In relation to the evaluation of the contemporaneous note, the judge said as follows:

> "*71 I turn to the evidence of Dr Johnson. He did not purport to have a clear recollection of the consultation but depended heavily upon his clinical note of the consultation, and his standard practice. As a contemporaneous record that Dr Johnson was duty bound to make, that record is obviously worthy of careful consideration. However, that record must be judged alongside the other evidence in the action. The circumstances in which it was created do not of themselves prevent it being established by other evidence that that record is in fact inaccurate.*"

On the facts, the judge preferred the defendant's evidence. He noted discrepancies in the parents' accounts and noted that their evidence had become more detailed as the litigation progressed.

*Shaw v Stead* [2019] EWHC 520 (QB) is a very recent decision where Yip J gave consideration to the weight to be placed upon contemporaneous medical records. The claimant, a teaching assistant, had sustained an injury after being kicked by a pupil. She had been knocked over and had twisted her back. She went on to develop cauda equina. By the time she saw the defendant, it was two days after the initial accident. There was a significant dispute of fact between the claimant and defendant as to what was said at that consultation. The defendant's note recorded that there were "no red flags". The claimant's evidence was that she attended the consultation in a wheelchair, her blood pressure, pulse and temperature were not checked. Her evidence was also that by the time of the consultation, she had urinary issues and weakness in her legs, both of which would have constituted red flags.

In relation to the weight to be attached to medical records, the judge said as follows:

> "*28 It is important when considering their evidence to look closely at the medical records. Ms Campbell-Clause urges that this is the most reliable source of evidence. There is though a balance to be struck. On the one hand the notes contain a contemporaneous record. They are not affected by hindsight and/or the passage of time. On the other hand, the authors of the notes have not been called and there has been no testing of the content. Very often medical records do provide the best evidence of what was happening at the time. However, they are not infallible, and they must be weighed and tested just as other evidence is. There are in this case some internal inconsistencies within the notes.*"

There is therefore no presumption as a matter of law that medical notes are likely to be more accurate than the recollection of witnesses. However, for the various reasons mentioned in the above passage, in the ordinary course of events, they are more likely to be accurate than a recollection by a witness, which may first have been rendered to writing some years after the event.

In sepsis and meningitis cases, it is therefore critically important that the relevant medical notes are obtained at an early stage, and they are put to the claimant (and/or their family, if appropriate). If there is a discrepancy between the claimant's recollection and the notes, the questions are:

a) Is the claimant misremembering the event? If they are uncertain in their recollection, and are swayed by the contents of the notes, or if there are obvious inaccuracies or discrepancies in the claimant's account, then this must be considered. It would be prudent to explore this very carefully in light of the weight that most judges would tend to attach to the contemporaneous records.

b) Is there a logical explanation for the discrepancy between the two accounts? There are numerous ways in which what appears at first to be a discrepancy can be explained:

    i. There may have been multiple consultations happening on the same day, and there may be confusion as to which was the key consultation;

    ii. In an illness where symptoms are progressing, claimants may be focusing on the eventual presentation rather than the initial one;

    iii. Particularly in the context of an acute episode on a busy ward or unit, notes may be written up retrospectively. It can sometimes be unclear whether the time of the note is the time at which it was made, or the time of the events it describes.

c) Is the note inaccurate? In some cases, this will be easier to prove than in others. Where, for instance, there are entries on either side that suggest that certain symptoms were (or must have been) present by a certain time, and such a symptom is absent from the index consultation record, that will be very good evidence to support the claimant's case.

From a claimant's point of view, if the accuracy of a contemporaneous medical record is to be challenged, it is best to identify the issue early on. It would be advisable to point out in the Letter of Claim which record (or records) are inaccurate, and, if it is possible to do so, set out a positive case, referring to such evidence as will be relied upon, so as to challenge the note.

It will normally be the case that where there is a factual dispute between the parties, there will be some risk on either side, that may be reflected in the parties' valuations of the case (or approach to compromise).

Aside from issues of accuracy, when considering the notes, one should be looking to consider the following points, where relevant:

a) In general terms, has any relevant guideline (whether national or local) been complied with?

b) When is the first record that the correct diagnosis is being considered? Could and should this have occurred sooner?

c) Ought a lumbar puncture (the test for meningitis, which involves the collection of CSF) to have been performed? If so, by when? If it has not been performed, is there a rational basis to explain that, which will generally be (i) that there is a presumed diagnosis of meningitis and the claimant has been treated accordingly, or (ii) there is a contra-indication for performing an LP.

d) In the case of sepsis secondary to pneumonia ought a chest x-ray to have been performed? If so, by when?

e) Is there regular and appropriate monitoring of clinical observations?

f) What medications have been given, and when? In a sepsis or meningitis claim, a key question is likely to be whether antibiotics have been started at the appropriate time. A question which will need to be considered by the breach and causation experts is what was the latest reasonable time for commencing (usually intravenous) antibiotics, and what would the outcome have been if that had occurred?

g) Has there been appropriate escalation to senior review? This is usually particularly problematic during night-time admission, when for the most part, consultants are not present unless called in by their registrars.

h) Has there been appropriate inter-disciplinary consultation or referral? There may be a need for microbiological, neurological, infectious diseases or ophthalmic review (to give but a few examples). There may be a need to seek specialist input from outside the treating hospital. In the case of critically ill children there may be a need to consult with an acute transfer service for critically ill children. There may have been a need to transfer to an intensive care unit (ICU). Did this happen at the appropriate time?

i) Be aware that once antibiotics are started, that will impact on the results of any cultures thereafter (i.e. it may not be possible to detect the relevant bacteria as the antibiotics may have killed them off).

It will make the job much easier if the records can be properly organised and paginated, and if a detailed chronology is prepared.

Once that preliminary evidence has been obtained, if it appears that there is a good case on breach of duty, it will be necessary to obtain preliminary reports from experts in breach of duty and causation. In most cases, a solicitor or barrister is (unless medically trained) unlikely to be able to make any proper assessment on causation without the assistance of an expert. Further, whilst potential breaches of duty may be identified, it is not until the appropriate expert on breach (be it GP, Emergency medicine, paediatrics, or surgical specialty, as the case may be) has reported that the true nature of the case will be understood.

The following abbreviations may be used in the notes:

| | |
|---|---|
| ABC | Airway, breathing, circulation |
| AVPU | Alert, voice, pain, unresponsive |
| BP | Blood pressure |
| BPM | Beats per minute |
| CRP | C-Reactive protein (a marker of infection) |
| CRT | Capillary refill time |
| CSF | Cerebrospinal fluid |
| CT | Computed tomography (a type of scan) |
| CVS | Cardiovascular system |
| CXR | Chest x-ray |
| ECG | Electrocardiogram |
| ED | Emergency department |
| ETT | Endotracheal tube |
| FBC | Full blood count |
| FFP | Fresh frozen plasma |
| GCS | Glasgow coma scale |
| HR | Heartrate |
| ICP | Intracranial pressure |
| INR | International normalised ratio (coagulation marker) |
| IO | Intraosseous |
| IV | Intravenous |
| LP | Lumbar puncture |
| MD | Meningococcal disease |

| | |
|---|---|
| NG | Nasogastric |
| PICU | Paediatric intensive care unit |
| RICP | Raised intracranial pressure |
| RR | Respiratory rate |
| T | Temperature |
| URTI | Upper respiratory tract infection |
| WCC | White blood cell count |

# CHAPTER SIX
# EXPERTS

As in most clinical negligence litigation, the case will be very heavily dependent on the expert evidence.

Many (or perhaps, most) of the experts practising within this field are well familiar with the legal tests they have to apply. However, it is not unusual to see a report which is couched in language that would not satisfy a judge, or else where certain key matters have not been considered at all, particularly where there are difficult causation issues, with a need to consider (a) a non-negligent timeline (or timelines, if there are alternative cases on breach), (b) the claimant's prognosis 'but for' the negligence, particularly bearing in mind any underlying or pre-existing illness.

## The Letter of Instruction

The best practice is to include a summary of the relevant legal principles in the letter of instruction, together with a list of the questions that are most relevant. The expert should also be asked to perform a detailed review of the medical notes and set out any breaches of duty they consider relevant. They should also be asked whether they consider any other disciplines of expert are needed to report on breach and causation.

There is a tendency for some experts to answer only the questions they are asked directly. It is therefore important to ensure that the instruction is sufficiently wide in scope that the expert understands the need to give thorough and detailed consideration to all relevant matters, including those which the solicitors may not know the significance of without the expert's assistance.

However experienced the expert, it will be worth reminding them of the following within the letter of instruction:

Breach of duty

(1) The question of breach of duty will be determined on *Bolam* and *Bolitho* principles. The key questions are therefore (a) was there an act or omission which fell below a proper standard according to a responsible body of medical opinion within the field? Put another way, an act or omission is negligent if no reasonable doctor would have acted in that way, and (b) even if the doctor has acted in accordance with a body of medical opinion, is that body of medical opinion logical and reasonable?

(2) In considering the standard to be applied to the individual doctor, this is to be judged according to the post they are filling, rather than their individual experience or length of service (*Wilsher v Essex Area Health Authority* [1987] QB 730). However, there are some skills, such as the taking of a history in A&E, which is a basic skill and in which all doctors, whatever their post, must be equally competent (*FB v Princess Alexandra Hospital NHS Trust* [2017] EWCA Civ 334).[1]

Causation

(3) In general terms, the question on causation is what was the impact on the claimant of the breach of duty, in terms of harm, damage or injury. This is to be measured on the balance of probabilities. Put another way: had there not been the relevant breach, and had the claimant received proper and appropriate care, what is the outcome likely on balance to have been?

(4) It may be helpful (particularly in time-sensitive cases such as those involving sepsis and meningitis) to set out clearly what the non-negligent timeline would be. If the expert's opinion leads them to conclude that there are alternative cases on breach and

---

1 See further below at p.76. There is some doubt about whether this reasoning can be correct.

causation, then it may be necessary to set out multiple hypothetical timelines.

(5) Is there a difficulty in determining on the balance of probabilities whether the negligence caused the injury? If so, is the expert able to say that the negligence made a material contribution to the injury? This exception to the general 'but for' causation rule only arises where medical science is unable to establish that 'but for' the negligence, the injury would not have occurred, provided the negligence made more than a negligible contribution to the injury (*Bailey v Ministry of Defence* [2008] EWCA Civ 883).

## Early Conference

An early conference with counsel and the experts will always be advisable in a sepsis or meningitis claim, preferably before the letter of claim is sent. This is because it is not until the issues have been carefully explored with the experts that their opinions can be:

a) Properly understood by the legal team;

b) Final, in that there may be challenges from either the other experts, counsel or the solicitor that have not been considered.

It is fairly common to see Letters of Claim drafted prior to any conference, where the allegations made do not cover the full scope of the claim that is to be advanced, or else, are worded in a manner which is not precisely at one with the expert's report in the form in which it is to be served. This can lead to difficulties and risks either advancing allegations in the Particulars of Claim of which the Defendant was not put on notice (which is risky from a costs point of view), or else having to serve a supplemental or second Letter of Claim.

There is a huge advantage to seeing the experts together. There are various reasons for this. Firstly, experts are not infallible. Having colleagues from other relevant disciplines present to challenge or question their views can be very important, if only to identify any weaknesses in the case, that may not have been appreciated. Secondly, whilst the experts are themselves independent, the process of presenting a case is a team effort. When one expert slightly alters or amends their opinion (perhaps following a challenge from counsel), that is likely to have a knock-on effect on the other experts, in terms of the facts and matters on which they are required to comment. It is for this reason that dealing with such matters in conference is more efficient and productive than writing to experts individually with written queries on initial reports.

In cases where there appears to be a factual discrepancy between the claimant's (or the claimant's family's) recollection and what is recorded in the contemporaneous notes, the experts should be used to test whether both versions are plausible, and if they are both plausible, which is more likely.

As an example of using an expert to challenge or corroborate conflicting evidence, in *Pringle v Nestor Prime Care Services* [2014] EWHC 1308 (QB),[2] which is a case involving meningococcal septicaemia, an ambulance crew had recorded the claimant's respiratory rate as 29/min at a time when she was extremely tachycardic (186 bpm) and was developing a meningococcal rash. The expert's view was that this record was implausible, which was accepted by the judge.

It is almost invariably the case that experts should have seen each other's reports by the time of the conference. Although there are some cases where it is preferable that the expert forms an independent view without the possible contamination of that view by seeing another expert's report in advance, even in such cases, by the time of the conference (in order for it to be as productive as possible), experts should usually have been provided with all reports.

2 See further below at p.70.

It is also good practice to have a draft set of allegations of breach and causation, whether in the form of draft Particulars of Claim or a draft Letter of Claim to function as an agenda.

Comments on the Letter of Response

After the Letter of Response is received, it is advisable to ask for the experts to provide detailed comments on any denials. It is probable that the letter will have been drafted with the input of an expert. As such, any denial contained within it is likely to form the basis of any defence if the claim is litigated.

Most sepsis, meningitis and meningococcal disease cases in which a dispute arises as to breach of duty will involve a dispute of fact. This is because national guidelines are so clear that if certain signs or symptoms are present, there is little doubt as to what the treatment will be.

Further conference

In most of these claims, it will be proportionate to have a second conference after the exchange of medical evidence but prior to the experts' meetings. By this time, the issues in the case should have crystallised, and it should be relatively clear what matters remain in dispute between the parties.

Experts' Meeting

It is advisable (and indeed, is normally directed by the Court) to provide the experts in each discipline with an agenda to facilitate their joint discussions. In a recent clinical negligence case,[3] Yip J expressed disappointment at a joint statement of 60 pages in length, which did not attempt to narrow the issues. She laid the blame on the legal representatives for failing to agree a single agenda, and failing to focus on the real issues. The joint statement is plainly a document of tremendous importance. In most cases, however, the experts will not stray beyond

3 *Saunders v Central Manchester University Hospitals NHS Foundation Trust* [2018] EWHC 343 (QB)

the agenda, and as such the joint statement can only be as good as the agenda.

It is advisable for an agenda to ask the specific questions on which the Court will require the experts' opinions, and to focus in on any areas of disagreement that are apparent from the experts' reports. If, for example, there is a disagreement on the relevance of, or views expressed within a journal article, it may be helpful to have a specific question referring to that article and requiring the experts pithily to explain their position. No genuine area of disagreement ought to be left until trial to resolve. The agenda should enable the experts clearly and concisely to express the key areas of agreement and disagreement.

It can be helpful to show a draft agenda to the experts to ensure that they consider all key issues are covered.

Questions ought to be phrased neutrally. If they are so phrased, and if the questions are relevant, there is no reason why the agenda ought not to be agreed.

# CHAPTER SEVEN
# THE INQUEST

It is beyond the scope of this book to give an in-depth consideration to the law of inquests.

However, due to the high incidence of fatalities in cases arising from sepsis, meningitis and meningococcal disease, any lawyer undertaking work in this area ought to give careful thought to how the inquest may bolster any proposed civil claim.

It is also very often the case that a bereaved family will first approach or instruct a solicitor in anticipation of the inquest hearing. There will often be insufficient time to obtain supportive expert evidence in advance of the inquest, and even in those cases with good prospects of success, there is often doubt as to whether the costs of the inquest will be recoverable. As a broad rule, where evidence is gathered at the inquest which is then used in a civil claim, the costs of the inquest (apart from pure inquest costs, such as submissions on inquest procedure) will be recoverable from the tortfeasor as part of a successful civil action.[1]

In any case involving an "unnatural death" (section 1(2) of the Coroners and Justice Act 2009), the coroner must hold an inquest.

An unnatural death is one "where it was wholly unexpected and it would not have occurred but for some culpable human failing" (*R v HM Coroner Inner London ex parte Touche* [2001] QB 1206).

## Scope

The statutory purpose of an inquest is to consider four questions, as set out in section 5 of the CJA 2009:

1 *Gibson's Settlement Trusts, Re* [1981] Ch 179, *Roach v Home Office* [2009] EWHC 312 (QB)

(1) Who the deceased was.

(2) How the deceased came by his or her death.

(3) When the deceased came by his or her death.

(4) Where the deceased came by his or her death.

The second question of 'how' is ordinarily where most of the evidence will lie, and where there is greatest scope for the representatives of the bereaved family to seek relevant answers.

In cases where Article 2 of the European Convention on Human Rights (ECHR) is engaged, which provides for the right to life to be protected by law, the question of 'how' is broadened to "by what means and in what broad circumstances did the deceased die" (*R (Middleton) v West Somerset Coroner* [2004] UKHL 10).

The law on whether article 2 is engaged against a clinical negligence background is as set out by Smith LJ in *R (Humberstone) v Legal Services Commission* [2010] EWCA Civ 1479:

> "*58 I would summarise [the judge's] by saying that article 2 imposes an obligation on the state to set up a judicial system which enables any allegation of possible involvement by a state agent to be investigated. That obligation may be satisfied in this country by criminal or civil proceedings, an inquest and even disciplinary proceedings or any combination of those procedures. This obligation envisages the provision of a facility available to citizens and not an obligation proactively to instigate an investigation. Only in limited circumstances (I depart from Richards J only so far as to decline to call them exceptional) will there be a specific obligation proactively to conduct an investigation. Those limited circumstances arise where the death occurs while the deceased is in the custody of the state or, in the context of allegations against hospital authorities, where the allegations are of a systemic nature such as the failure to provide suitable facilities or adequate staff or appropriate systems of operation. They*

> *do not include cases where the only allegations are of "ordinary" medical negligence.*"
>
> (Emphasis added)

Coroners are alive and resistant to any attempts to 'dress up' ordinary negligence as systemic failures on the pretext of coming within article 2 simply in order to widen the scope of the inquiry.

However, the requirement to investigate systemic failures and to enquire into whether neglect contributed to a death means that "*there will often be little difference in practice between*" traditional inquests and those where the full Article 2 obligation arises (*R (Takoushis) v HM Coroner for Inner North London* [2006] 1 WLR 461, para 43-47).

The scope of the inquiry (as set at any Pre-Inquest Review, or otherwise) ought to be sufficiently broad to consider all matters relevant to the question of 'how' the deceased died. It is settled law that the inquiry is not restricted to the "last link in the chain of causation".[2]

Evidence

The inquest hearing will be the only opportunity prior to trial of questioning the witnesses of fact who were present in the hours leading up to the death, and who made the vital decisions. It is a very valuable opportunity to question the healthcare professionals who will be the key witnesses in the litigation.

It should be borne in mind that pursuant to rule 22 of The Coroners (Inquests) Rules 2013, (1) a witness is not obliged to answer any questions tending to incriminate him or her, and further (2) the coroner must inform a witness who is asked such a question that they do not have to answer it.

---

2 *R v Inner West London Coroner, Ex p Dallaglio* [1994] 4 All ER 139, approved by the Court of Appeal in *R (Sreedharan) v HM Coroner for the County of Greater Manchester & Ors* [2013] EWCA Civ 181

This must be understood against the background of section 10(2) of the CJA 2009, which prevents a coroner from making a determination which is framed so as to determine any question of criminal or civil liability.

That does not mean that questions which might lead to an incriminating answer should not be *asked* (there being no rule against this).

It is suggested that the evidence of the relevant medical professionals at the inquest provides the following opportunities:

(a) It is an opportunity to gauge to what extent the relevant medical professionals remember the index events, and to test the accuracy of any such recollection;

(b) If there are gaps in the evidence (i.e. explaining why parts of the notes or unclear or incomplete, or why certain protocols or guidelines were not followed when it appears they ought to have been), those gaps should be properly explored;

(c) If there has been a serious incident report, the author (or one of the authors) of the report will usually be called to attend to give evidence. With regard to this witness, the coroner will be most interested in making sure any lessons have been learned. However, they are likely to have reviewed more evidence than the family have had access to by that time (including undisclosed accounts of all medical professionals involved in the care). As such, their evidence can be extremely valuable, not purely in terms of lessons learnt, but in terms of understanding precisely what occurred and why.

Conclusion

Pursuant to rule 27 of the Coroners (Inquests) Rules 2013, it is not permitted to address the coroner on the facts. However, the coroner will ask for submissions on the appropriate conclusion (formerly known as the 'verdict'), and such submissions cannot be made without some reference to the facts.

There are three conclusions which are most likely to be considered in cases involving sepsis and meningitis deaths:

(A) Neglect

Neglect is not truly a 'short-form' conclusion (i.e. it is not one of the suggested short-form conclusions set out on the Form2: Record of an Inquest), but a rider that is normally attached to a narrative verdict. It is not the same as negligence, and there will often be cases where although there appears to be negligence (or even where there has been an admission of liability prior to the inquest), there is no finding of neglect.

The definition of neglect is found in the case of *R v HM Coroner for North Humberside and Scunthorpe Ex p Jamieson* [1995] QB 1:

> "*Neglect in this context means a gross failure to provide adequate nourishment or liquid, or provide or procure basic medical attention or shelter or warmth for someone in a dependent position (because of youth, age, illness or incarceration) who cannot provide it for himself. Failure to provide medical attention for a dependent person whose physical condition is such as to show that he obviously needs it may amount to neglect. So it may be if it is the dependent person's medical condition which obviously called for medical attention… In both cases the crucial consideration will be what the dependent person's condition, whether physical or mental, appeared to be.*"

In summary, the essential ingredients are:

- The deceased was a dependent person
- A gross failure
- Failure to provide basic attention

- A clear and direct causal connection between the failure and the death.

Neglect is often made out in cases where there has been a failure by the medical team to take seriously the concerns of the deceased or their family, which has led to the seriousness of the condition not being appreciated in a timely and appropriate manner.

(B) Unlawful killing

This conclusion will rarely arise in the context of a death resulting from sepsis or meningitis. In common with a conclusion of suicide, the standard of proof is 'beyond a reasonable doubt'. The test for gross negligence manslaughter would have to be made out, which is a breach of duty so gross that the breach was beyond the mere inadvertence in relation to the obvious and important matter which the duty demanded the individual should address (*R v Adamako* [1995] AC 171 (HL)).

It has been said that in a medical background "mistakes, even very serious mistakes, and errors of judgment, even very serious errors of judgment, and the like, are nowhere near enough for a crime as serious as manslaughter to be committed" (*R v Misra* [2005] 1 Cr App Rep 21 [25] (CA)).

It is hard to contemplate a set of facts whereby this would be an appropriate conclusion. However, it is noted that there was a recent case of conviction of a doctor for gross negligence manslaughter arising from a sepsis background, where such a conclusion would have been open.[3]

(C) Accident

This conclusion is appropriate in cases where (a) neither the acts causing the death, nor the consequences of those acts were intended; or (b) the death was an unintended consequence of actions that were themselves deliberate.

3 The unsuccessful appeal against that conviction can be found at *R v Bawa-Garba* [2016] EWCA Crim 1841.

When considering whether to record a conclusion of either natural causes or accident, in the context of a hospital death, the key question is whether at the time of the unsuccessful treatment, the deceased is likely to die in any event, or whether there was still an opportunity to save him or her at the time of the treatment.[4] Accordingly, if the treatment caused or contributed to the death, accident will be the appropriate conclusion.

(D) Narrative conclusion

Alternatively, the coroner may record a narrative conclusion, with or without a 'short-form' conclusion attached. This is mandatory in inquests where Article 2 is engaged. However, it is very common for coroners to record a narrative conclusion in hospital death inquests, as short-form conclusions typically fail to do justice to the facts.

The coroner may be critical in his or her findings. However, pursuant to section 10(2) of the CJA 2009, no determination should be framed so as to appear to determine either criminal or civil liability. With reliance on, and reference to case law, the former Chief Coroner HHJ Peter Thornton QC gave the following guidance on the use of judgmental language in Guidance Note No.17[5] (albeit this was in the context of narrative conclusions to Article 2 inquests, but there is no reason why the same guidance would not apply to all inquests where a narrative conclusion is given):

> "*52. Permitted judgmental words include 'inadequate', 'inappropriate', 'insufficient', 'lacking', 'unsuitable', 'unsatisfactory', and 'failure'... Words denoting causation such as 'because' and 'contributed to' are permissible.*

4 *R v Birmingham Coroner Ex p Benton* [1997] 8 Med LR 362.

5 https://www.judiciary.uk/wp-content/uploads/2013/09/guidance-no-17-conclusions.pdf

> *53. On the other hand words which suggest civil liability such as 'negligence', 'breach of duty', 'breach of article 2' and 'careless' are not permitted as they may breach Section 10(2), 2009 Act.*"

Positive or negative findings by a coroner at an inquest may be a useful indication for the parties of how a judge would be likely to assess the same evidence in a civil trial. However, a narrative verdict from an inquest is not admissible evidence in a civil trial,[6] although the evidence may be admitted under Civil Evidence Act notices.[7]

---

6 *Daniel v St George's Healthcare NHS Trust* [2016] EWHC 23 (QB).

7 Under section 2 of the Civil Evidence Act 1995.

# CHAPTER EIGHT
# DAMAGES

There is such a wide range of outcomes in claims arising from sepsis, meningitis and meningococcal disease, that it is difficult to provide too much general guidance on damages.

This brief chapter will simply refer to the relevant heads of loss that will need to be investigated and refer in broad terms to the sorts of awards that may be made.

## General Damages

In all cases, the Judicial College Guidelines (currently in the 14th Edition), will need to be considered.

In cases resulting in brain injury, it would be advisable to consider Chapter 3 of the Guidelines in full. The brackets range from:

- Category 3(A)(d) 'less severe': **£13,430 to £37,760**[1]
- Category 3(A)(c) 'Moderate': **£37,760 to £192,090** (with the award being determined according to extent of intellectual deficit, employability and epilepsy risk)[2]
- Category 3(A)(b) 'Moderately severe': **£192,090 to £247,280**
- Category 3(A)(a) 'Very severe': **£247,280 to £354,260**

---

1 NB: when referring to brackets within the Guidelines, the figures given are inclusive of a 10% uplift pursuant to *Simmons v Castle* [2013] 1 WLR 1239, on the basis that there is no pre-LASPO funding arrangement in place. It is noted that there will be some cases involving children or protected parties where funding arrangement were entered prior to 1 April 2013, in which case the figures must be reduced by 10%.

2 NB: within the Guidelines, this category is sub-divided into three further subcategories.

For limb amputations arising from septicaemia, the following are example of what the Guidelines provide:

- Category 7(E)(b)(iii) 'Below elbow amputation': **£84,310 to £96,150**
- Category 7(I)(d) 'Amputation of index and middle and/or ring finger': **£54,280 to £79,560**
- Category 7(I)(j) 'Total loss of index finger': **Around £16,420**
- Category 7(I)(p) 'Amputation of little finger': **£7,580 to £10,730**
- Category 7(I)(u) 'Loss of thumb': **£31,140 to £48,080**
- Category 7(P)(a) 'Amputation of both feet': **£148,540 to £176,660**
- Category 7(P)(b) 'Amputation of one foot': **£73,620 to £96,150**
- Category 7(Q)(b) 'Amputation of the great toe': **Around £27,450**
- Category 7(Q)(c) 'Severe toe injuries':[3] **£12,050 to £18,480**

Deafness is a common injury resulting from meningitis, where the relevant bracket is likely to be:

- Category 5(B)(c) 'Total loss of hearing in one ear': **£27,450 to £39,940**

The awards in fatal cases are predictably lower, with general damages normally assessed in reference to Chapter 1, where in most cases of rapid decline followed by death, the relevant category will be:

3 Including amputations to toes other than the great toe.

- Category 1(D) 'Immediate unconsciousness / death within one week': **£1,200 to £2,450**

The cases of greatest value will be those where a claimant has been left with significant brain damage, and/or severe disability through amputations. Cases of neonatal meningitis may lead to severe cerebral palsy.

## Special damages

As in all personal injury and clinical negligence claims, lawyers acting for the claimant will want to investigate:

i. **Loss of earnings**. In some cases, there will be no residual earnings capacity. In others, that capacity will be severely diminished. In many cases, a claimant may be disabled under the Equality Act 2010, such that (in cases where it is appropriate to calculate future losses on a conventional Ogden 7 basis) the multiplier for residual earnings will be significantly discounted to reflect such disability. There may also be a claim for loss of pension.

ii. **Care and assistance.** In cases of significant brain damage, there may be a very significant care requirement (for instance, in cases of neonatal meningitis giving rise to cerebral palsy). The Court will look to consider (i) what the claimant's needs are, (ii) whether the model of care chosen by, or for, the claimant is reasonable, and (iii) what the reasonable costs of meeting the claimant's needs are (in accordance with *Sowden v Lodge* [2004] EWCA Civ 1370). In many cases, it will be appropriate for this to be ordered or settled by way of an index-linked periodical payments order (PPO).[4]

iii. **Case management.** This is likely to be required for a claimant with severe disabilities, such that the claimant will have a profes-

4 Generally, the Annual Survey of Hours and Earnings (ASHE) for the occupational group of care assistants and home carers (classification 6115), known as 'ASHE 6115'.

sional person to coordinate their care and other needs. As with care, this is commonly ordered or settled by way of a PPO.

iv. **Accommodation.** Subject to the claimant's physical disabilities, there may be a need for new or adapted accommodation. The leading case on the calculation of accommodation claims is *Roberts v Johnstone*,[5] pursuant to which a claimant can recover only an annual sum in reference to an assumed rate of interest on the capital expenditure, applied to a lifetime multiplier (in addition to any adaptation costs, subject to a deduction for value added to the property by such adaptations). Under a negative discount rate (which is presently at -0.25%), the *Roberts v Johnstone* approach produces a nil award for future accommodation. The following three points should be noted:

   a. The Court of Appeal has adjourned the appeal *Swift v Carpenter*[6] which seeks to challenge *Roberts v Johnstone* in order for further evidence to be presented. The appeal will now be heard in March 2020.

   b. When parties are considering accommodation for the purposes of settlement, there are various potential alternatives, including a charge over a property, PPOs based upon the notional cost of commercial borrowing, a lifetime trust in a property purchased by a defendant, or sums or PPOs to fund rented accommodation.

v. **Aids and equipment.** The claimant will be entitled to recover such aids and equipment as are reasonably required to put them back in the position they would have been in but for the negligence. Obvious examples are mobility devices, hoists, exercise equipment, and adapted kitchen equipment. Such items usually require periodic replacement, such that periodic multipliers should be applied. So long as the item is reasonable, the fact

5 [1989] QB 878.

6 First instance judgment: [2018] EWHC 2060 (QB).

that the defendant may be able to identify a cheaper alternative is probably not relevant (*A v Powys Health Board* [2007] EWHC 2996 (QB)).

vi. **Prosthetics.** The principles applied to recovery for prosthetics are in effect no different from those applied to aids and equipment. Again, the claimant must prove reasonable requirement and reasonable cost. Where the claimant is a child, more frequent replacements are likely to be required as the claimant grows.

vii. **Treatment and therapies.** The claimant will be able to recover for future treatment and therapy costs which are real rather than fanciful or speculative. Where there is a real, but low chance of treatment being required, an award should be made based on the chance of the treatment being needed (as in *Finnie v South Devon Health Care NHS Foundation Trust* [2014] EWHC 4333 (QB), where an award was made on the 22.5% chance of needing surgery relating to a colostomy). The claimant may claim for the cost of private therapies or treatment even if they are available on the NHS, if on the balance of probabilities, such treatment or therapies will be privately obtained.[7]

viii. **Lost years.** Where, as a result of a reduction in life expectancy, an adult claimant suffers a financial loss (i.e. loss of earnings or pension), a claim can be made (pursuant to *Pickett v BRE* [1980] AC 136 (HL)). The claim is calculated by taking the claimant's net earnings and deducting from that the cost of the claimant's living expenses. The starting point is usually 50%. That multiplicand can then be applied to an appropriate multiplier, which will need to be discounted or enhanced for accelerated receipt, and discounted for contingencies. Where the claimant is a child, there is Court of Appeal authority against such claim being allowed (*Croke v Wiseman* [1982] 1 WLR 71 (CA)). However, this decision has been doubted by the Court

7 Pursuant to section 2(4) of the Law Reform (Personal Injuries) Act 1948.

of Appeal since (notably in *Iqbal v Whipps Cross University NHS Trust* [2007] EWCA Civ 1190). Strictly, the matter will need to be taken to the Supreme Court for the law to change, but such claims should nevertheless be pleaded, as they will often be settled in the claimant's favour.

Fatal cases

In fatal claims, there will be different considerations. Many such claims will involve children, and as such, the main heads of loss are likely to be for general damages for PSLA, bereavement damages,[8] and funeral costs.

For fatal claims involving adults, the elements claimed under the Law Reform (Miscellaneous Provisions) Act 1934 will be those elements relating to losses suffered by the deceased before their death and any expenses incurred by the estate itself. These claims are generally straightforward and are no different to claims for damages in non-fatal cases.

There is often argument in relation to probate fees, and any inquest costs.

(a) **Probate fees.** Whilst the 1934 Act does not specifically allow for recovery of probate costs, and such claims have been disallowed in some cases (e.g. *Mosson v Spousal (London) Ltd* [2016] EWHC 1429 (QB)), where the grant of probate has been obtained in order to bring the action, then it is possible that the fees can be recovered as part of the costs of litigation.

(b) **Inquest costs.** The only basis for recovery of inquest costs (other than in very rare cases where the bereaved family successfully applied for legal aid) will be as costs which are of an incidental to civil proceedings. There is, however, no basis on which these costs may be recovered as damages in a fatal case.

8 Currently set at £12,980, pursuant to section 1A(3) of the Fatal Accidents Act 1976 (as amended).

Where there is a dependent under the Fatal Accidents Act 1976, there may be claims for the following:

(a) **Loss of services dependency.** Where the deceased provided services in terms of domestic care, housework and gardening, for example, the starting point for what has been lost will be the commercial cost of replacing such services, so long as that cost is reasonable.

(b) **Loss of financial dependency.** This claim in calculated based on the earnings of the deceased less whatever proportion of those earnings the deceased would have spent on themselves. The general presumption (which can be displaced by evidence in appropriate cases) is that an individual with dependent children will spend 25% of their income on themselves, and that an individual who is married but has no dependent children will spend a third of their income on themselves. The approach is to pool income from the married couple, multiply by the dependency percentage, then deduct the surviving spouse's income.

(c) **Loss of intangible benefits.** In some cases, the Court will make an additional award to dependants to reflect that services provided by a parent or spouse includes intangible benefits which cannot be provided by a professional. Such sum is usually between £2,500 and £5,000 in value.

Whether funeral expenses are recovered on behalf of the dependents under the 1976 Act or the estate under the 1934 Act will depend on who paid for them. Funeral expenses must be reasonable in all the circumstances.

Where close relatives have suffered sudden psychiatric injury as a result of the negligence, there may be scope for secondary victim claims, although that is a subject beyond the scope of this book.

# CHAPTER NINE
# CASEBOOK

Because cases in this area will always be fact specific, it is helpful to see real examples from the reported cases. It is obvious that there will be many more cases where the issues were not as contentious which were settled out of court.

The below is a brief review of key cases from within the past 10 years.

*Knott v Leading* [2010] EWHC 1827 (QB)

The facts

On 19 April 2000 the defendant GP visited the claimant (then aged 11 years) at home. The claimant's case was that three petechial spots were present on her neck at this time. The defendant's evidence was that only one spot was present on the claimant's neck, and it was non-petechial. The following day, the claimant was admitted to hospital with meningococcal disease, as a result of which she developed profound deafness, hearing loss, tinnitus and vestibular dysfunction.

The issues

The one issue to be determined was whether at the time of the visit, the claimant had three non-blanching petechiae on her neck. If so, she ought to have been referred immediately to A&E, where she would have been treated with antibiotics which would have stopped the progression of the meningococcal disease early enough so as to avoid long-term damage. If the defendant was correct, there was no need for referral.

The judgment

The judge preferred the evidence of the defendant to that of the claimant's parents. This was in part due to inconsistencies between their recollections and what was recorded in the notes (such as the claimant's mother insisting that a telephone call was made to the GP of which there was no record). Most significantly, however, the paediatric experts agreed that the claimant's presentation at triage on 20 April could not be reconciled with the mother's description of the claimant's illness. The hospital records post-admission supported a fast-developing petechial rash late in the evening of 20 April, which was not consistent with the same rash having been present early on the afternoon of the previous day.

Learning points

This case is typical of a factual dispute, where careful consideration of the notes together with guidance from the experts ought to have alerted the claimant's advisors to the fact that her mother's recollection was improbable and not consistent with the usual development of meningococcal disease. It underlines the importance of a detailed and thorough review of the notes and an early conference.

### *Pringle v Nestor* [2014] EWHC 1308 (QB)

The facts

This was a meningococcal septicaemia case. the claimant was a two-year-old girl who was unwell in the evening of 16 November 2004 with high fever, vomiting and other symptoms. Shortly after midnight, her mother called her GP and was given the number for the defendant's 'out-of-hours' service. She had a 15-minute conversation with a triage nurse, who concluded that the claimant was probably suffering from an URTI. He did not arrange for admission to hospital or for a doctor to attend. The claimant developed a non-blanching rash and was admitted to hospital the next morning. She developed gangrene in both feet due to septicaemia, leading to the amputation of both feet. Unusually, there was a full recording and transcript available of the index telephone consultation.

The issues

Allegations of breach were advanced on the basis that the defendant should have arranged for the claimant's immediate admission to hospital or alternatively, have arrange for a home visit. The defendant accepted the second of these two points, but not the first. Causation was also disputed on the basis that even if there had been timely transfer and admission, that by the time the correct diagnosis had been made and treatment given, it would have been too late to avoid the amputations.

The judgment

The remaining issue on breach of duty (i.e. whether there should have been immediate ambulance transfer) was determined in the claimant's favour, largely in reference to the algorithm system the triage nurse was required to apply.

In terms of causation, the judge relied heavily on paediatric expert evidence in deciding what the likely progression of the disease is likely to have been. He accepted the claimant's case that had there been timely hospital admission, bacterial sepsis would have been a differential diagnosis, and IV antibiotics would have been started in sufficient time to avoid the amputations she suffered. Interestingly, he also held that if he was wrong about the primary case on causation, he would have allowed the claim on the basis of material contribution arguments in any event.

Learning points

On the key issue of the likely outcome had there been appropriate referral, this was simply a case of the judge preferring the claimant's expert over the defendant's expert. The key learning point, therefore, is in selecting the appropriate expert. In this case, that was a paediatric intensive care consultant with particular expertise in the pathophysiology and management of sepsis who had widely published on the subject, and who had the greater clinical experience of treating meningococcal disease.

*Coakley v Rosie* [2014] EWHC 1790 (QB)

The facts

The claimant was a 42-year-old woman who contracted bacterial meningitis. She started to feel unwell 29 December 2007, with flu-like symptoms. She stayed at home for a week thereafter. On 7 January 2008, the claimant's evidence was that she had developed a rash across the palm of her left hand, both lower arms and across her midriff. She arranged to see the defendant GP that afternoon. There was a factual dispute as to what was said and done at that appointment, however, it was agreed that the defendant had not required the claimant to undress, and had not checked her skin for signs of blanching. That evening, the claimant became unresponsive and appeared to choke on her own vomit. She was taken to hospital by ambulance and found ultimately to be suffering from meningococcal meningitis. She suffered total blindness and partial hearing loss.

The issues

A key issue of fact to be determined was whether the claimant's rash was non-blanching at the time of the consultation, or whether it was itchy and urticarial (i.e. hives). The experts agreed that itchy or urticarial rashes are not associated with meningitis, whereas non-blanching rashes are. In terms of causation, there was a dispute as to whether the claimant's injuries would have been avoided had the proper treatment been given.

The judgment

On the issue of breach of duty, the judge found as a fact that a meningococcal rash was present, which would have led to a high index of suspicion of meningitis, if properly seen or examined. On the issue of causation, the judge was unimpressed by the defendant's experts (in infectious disease, microbiology and neurology) and rejected their evidence that earlier antibiotics would have made no difference was totally unsupported.

Learning points

The mechanism on injury in this case was somewhat uncertain, as there was damage to the optic nerve which had probably been caused by the infection itself rather than simply through raised intracranial pressure. The key question was ultimately which experts were able to provide the explanation for whether or not this injury could have been prevented by earlier administration of antibiotics. Significantly, the judge found that none of the defendant's causation experts were able to explain themselves. Again, the issue comes back to the need for experts to be properly challenged in conference at an early stage and throughout the life of the claim. It is insufficient to simply have an opinion, particularly in the context of a rare or unusual injury. Opinions must either be supported by literature, or in reference to significant relevant knowledge and expertise gained in clinical practice.

## *W v Johnson [2015]* EWHC 276 (QB)

The facts

The claimant was four years old. On the afternoon 1 January 2010, his mother called NHS Direct and reported a temperature of 38.5°C, headache and vomiting. She was advised to bring him to an out-of-hours service, where he was examined by the defendant GP. The defendant noted a temperature of 39.4°C, the absence of a rash, and nothing else of note. He prescribed Calpol and Nurofen and advise the claimant's parents to return the next day if he was no better. The parents did not return, but on the evening of 2 January, took him to hospital, by which point it was too late for any effective treatment to be given. The claimant suffered severe neurological damage due to pneumococcal meningitis.

The issues

Breach of duty and causation were in dispute. There was a dispute of fact in that the claimant's parents alleged that at the time of the consultation, the claimant displayed symptoms of headache, fever and vomiting, which mandated immediate referral. The defendant denied this.

The judgment

The defendant's version was preferred.[1] The parents' version had become more detailed as the litigation had progressed, which was counter-intuitive. Further, there were too many highly corroborative accounts from friends and family, which led the judge to believe there had been an unsatisfactory degree of liaison between the witnesses. The judge found it hard to accept that if the claimant had presented in the condition described by his parents, that the defendant would not have done more. The claim was dismissed.

Learning points

To an extent, where there is a pure dispute of fact between the parties which cannot be resolved by pointing to physiological improbability or inconsistencies in the records, it will be difficult to anticipate the outcome before trial (which is an unsatisfactory state of affairs on both sides). The points that emerge from this case are (1) that obtaining a long list of indirect witnesses to relay what was said at the time by witnesses who will give direct evidence, is unlikely to assist, even if (or perhaps especially if) it is highly corroborative, (2) in a case where a very high degree of negligence is asserted (i.e. a doctor ignoring textbook signs of meningitis), the evidence will have to be highly cogent in order to persuade a judge that it is likely on the balance of probabilities that it occurred, albeit that that threshold has been passed in other cases mentioned in this chapter, (3) most judges will approach any account that runs counter to the contemporaneous medical records with a degree of

1 See above at p.40.

scepticism unless there is good reason to doubt the accuracy of those records.[2]

## *XYZ (a child) v Maidstone and Tunbridge Wells NHS Trust* [2016] EWHC 2687 (QB)

The facts

The claimant was a two-year-old boy who had suffered febrile convulsions on several occasions in the past. On 21 May 2001, he had been unwell with a cold. On 22 May he went to nursery but was out of sorts in the afternoon and was collected by his mother and grandmother. He was given Calpol and ibuprofen. He refused his milk and would not settle. In the late evening he had a febrile fit. An ambulance was called, and he was taken to A&E. the claim concerned the treatment received from Dr F, a paediatric SHO.

Dr F performed what was undoubtedly a fairly detailed review (the totality of the contemporaneous note is set out in the judgment), but did not order blood tests, or arrange for senior review. At the time of the first review, the claimant had a temperature of 39.4°C and was tachycardic. Capillary refill time was less than two seconds, there was no rash and no neck stiffness. He was noted to be alert upon examination.

As a result of pneumococcal meningitis, the claimant suffered severe brain damage with a severe cognitive impairment, and a substantial loss of vision.

The issues

The case on breach of duty focused on two examinations by Dr F during the course of the night. The question was whether those examinations were adequate. The question on causation which flowed from that, was whether if they were not adequate, the claimant's care would have been any different if they had been.

2 See above at p.41.

The judgment

The judge relied heavily on the evidence from the expert microbiologists in considering the probable timeline for the development of the disease, and what symptoms are likely to have manifested at what time, the key issue being what ought to have been detectable at Dr F's two examinations. Based on that evidence, the judge came to the conclusion that whilst bacteraemia was present at the time, the inflammatory response (which causes the serious damage) had not yet started. He further found that the examinations were reasonable and there was no breach of duty in not ordering blood tests. Had there been a breach, causation would have been made out, in that antibiotics would have avoided any serious injury being sustained.

Learning points

It is to be borne in mind that times have changed in the treatment of both meningitis and sepsis since the facts of this case. All the relevant NICE guidelines have come into place after this incident. It may be the case, therefore, that the issue of breach of duty would be resolved differently today, in that current guidelines require a more interventionist approach, with a low threshold for the administration of antibiotics and blood screening.

### *FB v Rana* [2017] EWCA Civ 334

The facts

The claimant was a 13-month-old child who had been unwell since 18 September 2003. On 29 September she was taken to hospital by ambulance at 04:00. The crew recorded a history from the parents that her eyes had been rolling around and she was very lethargic. The claimant was seen in A&E by an SHO who took a detailed history, but did not elicit the fact of the eyes rolling around. The trial judge appears to have accepted the SHO's evidence that she started with a relatively open question like "why are you here" and then followed up as she deemed fit. It was found as a fact that the parents would have volunteered the detail about the claimant's eyes rolling had they been asked. The SHO considered the claimant to be suffering from a probable URTI and discharged her. She returned in an ambulance later the same day, and a diagnosis of pneumococcal meningitis with multiple brain infarcts was made. She suffered permanent brain damage, with learning difficulties and profound deafness.

The issues

The SHO admitted as part of her evidence that had she known about the claimant's eyes rolling, she would have referred to paediatrics. The agreed evidence on causation was that had there been a paediatric referral, the claimant would have been treated with antibiotics and made a full recovery.

At first instance, the judge found that a more experienced doctor would have said something along the lines of "this child looks fine to me, how was she different earlier?" He concluded that the history taken by the SHO was reasonable, bearing in mind her experience.

On appeal, the claimant argued that history taking was a basic task that did not depend upon the experience or seniority of the doctor, and the judge had applied the wrong standard of care.

The judgment

The Court of Appeal accepted the claimant's arguments that a history taken by an SHO should be judged by the same standard as an experienced consultant. However (seeing off any serious prospect of a further appeal), the Court also found that the SHO was not even carried out to the expected standard of a competent SHO.

Learning points

Whilst the Court of Appeal's judgment has not been appealed, there must be some doubt as whether it is correct, insofar as it appears to depart from the law on standard of care as previously laid down in

*Wilsher v Essex AHA* [1987] 1 QB 730, in that it seeks to create an exception to the general rule that standard of care is to judged according to the post occupied by the medical professional.

Unless or until the point is considered further by the Supreme Court, claimants are in the advantageous position of being able to hold all doctors to a higher standard in relation to a "basic task" like history taking. It is not clear what, if any, further tasks would fall into this category, although obiter remarks mention "the delivery of a baby, the examination of a patient, the performing of surgery".

### *Keh v Homerton University Hospitals NHS Foundation Trust* [2019] EWHC 548 (QB)

The facts

This was a fatal sepsis case, brought by the husband of the deceased. The deceased was a 40-year-old woman who had attended hospital at 36 weeks and six days' gestation with concerns about her foetus. An induction of labour was commenced. However, as labour did not progress, she underwent an emergency caesarean section. Several days later, she developed signs of post-natal sepsis, and began receiving treatment in the form of antibiotics. She deteriorated and died as a result of sepsis. It was agreed that the infection had been introduced during the caesarean operation.

The issues

The claimant alleged that the deceased should have been offered an earlier planned caesarean section, due to increased risks from an emergency section as the deceased was 40 years old, overweight, and a Jehovah's Witness (and would therefore not accept blood transfusions), and that on balance, had this taken place, no infection would have developed (on *Chester v Afshar*[3] principles). There was also a question of whether a hysterectomy should have been offered.

3 [2004] UKHL 41.

### The judgment

The judge found that although the deceased should have been warned that she was at higher than normal risk of needing a caesarean section, that even if that risk had been communicated to her, she would probably have followed medical advice and opted for induction. There was no breach in not offering a caesarean section earlier than the defendant did, or from failing to offer or perform a hysterectomy.

### Learning points

Unlike most cases involving sepsis where the allegations centre on alleged failure to provide prompt or appropriate treatment, the claimant's case attempted to attack the fact that sepsis had been allowed to develop in the first place. The claimant faced a major difficulty in having to convince the court that the deceased would have gone against medical advice and opted to undergo an earlier caesarean section, had she been given the option. This argument rested to a significant degree on the claimant's evidence, who conceded during cross-examination that his wife would have followed medical advice.

# CHAPTER TEN
# PRACTICAL ADVICE

Every case is different, and the manner in which a case is to be run will depend on the facts, the evidence and the specific circumstances of each particular case. The following principles and pieces of practical advice arise from the learning points from the previous chapters and reported cases.

**Review the evidence**

This means taking full and detailed accounts from the claimant and/or their family members at the earliest opportunity, obtaining full medical records, including any root cause analysis or serious incident report, and any internal trust guidelines or protocols. Have the records sorted and paginated, and prepare a detailed chronology. Identify any inconsistencies between the claimant's account and the contemporaneous medical records so these can be investigated and dealt with, and any risk flagged up at the earliest opportunity.

**Instruct appropriate experts**

Every expert should be instructed on the presumption that they will have to give evidence at trial. That means that they will need to be a match for whoever may be instructed by the other side. It is therefore critically important that the experts have true expertise in the field. For instance, in a paediatric meningitis case, instructing a paediatrician with a special interest in infectious diseases who has published widely on meningitis and has considerable relevant clinical experience is preferable to a general paediatrician who does not have objectively verifiable expertise in meningitis.

Experts should be instructed at the earliest opportunity, and should be provided with a full set of the sorted and paginated notes. In cases where factual issues have been flagged, the experts should be made aware of this at the same time they are instructed, which will avoid multiple redrafts, and can also avoid them becoming fixated on a certain view in circumstances where that view is based on what may be a false premise.

## Early conference

In almost all cases, it will be advisable to have an early conference with counsel and experts on breach and causation. This is for the reasons set out above in detail within **Chapter Six: Experts.**[1]

## Look at your case critically

If any aspect of the case is difficult (particularly once it is known that such aspect is being challenged or contested) it is important to examine that aspect of the case with a critical eye. That means that where there is a discrepancy between a claimant's recollection and what is recorded in the notes, it is necessary to consider whether the claimant's version is (1) plausible and (2) probable.

Where there is a disagreement between your experts and the experts on the other side, it is not enough to simply have expert support. What is needed is expert support that is grounded in either objective data, or an opinion that is likely to be preferred. When considering whether an expert's opinion is likely to be preferred, the sorts of points to consider are:

i. does the expert have the relevant clinical experience to comment authoritatively?

ii. is the expert still in clinical practice? It is common to see experts reporting on breach who are no longer working within the NHS. That is inadvisable, particularly in relation to areas of medicine where practice standards are constantly changing.

1 See p.49.

iii. has the expert undertaken research in the relevant field (although judges can be wary of experts who are very specialist and who may be pioneers within a certain field, which may inhibit their objectivity when applying the *Bolam* standard)

iv. does one expert have an answer to the other expert's conflicting opinion, and is that answer reasoned, logical and otherwise consistent with his or her opinion?

v. has the expert applied the correct test?

vi. is the expert objective, and attempting to assist the Court?

### Letter of claim

In most cases, a conference ought to take place before this is served. In any event, the Letter of Claim is the best opportunity to secure an early admission. The case should be set out in detail. If, and to the extent that the claimant seeks to challenge any contemporaneous medical notes, this is the earliest opportunity to do so, and there is some tactical advantage in taking that opportunity. It will avoid the suggestion that the claimant is responding to the defendant's case, or that he or she is changing the story, having been caught out by unhelpful records. There is always advantage in advancing a positive case.

### Comments on letter of response

The letter of response will, most probably, have been drafted with the benefit of some expert input on the defendant's side. As such, in a case where breach or causation are disputed, this will be the first opportunity to consider the defendant's case. It is advisable for the claimant's solicitors to obtain comments from the experts on the letter of response, and to seek confirmation as to whether they remain supportive.

## Further conference

In most sepsis, meningitis or meningococcal disease cases, it will be reasonable and proportionate to have at least one further conference with the experts. In most cases this will take place after exchange of expert reports but prior to joint statements. In some cases (and where it is proportionate), there will be a need for a conference either before the pleadings are finalised or before the reports are served.

## Agenda

A good and focused agenda is absolutely vital in order for the experts' discussions to fulfil their potential and for a useful joint statement to be produced. Questions are to be phrased neutrally but should be specific, and should aim to elicit responses which will assist the Court by defining the nature of any disagreement, or alternatively, inducing the experts to find areas of agreement. Where an agenda refers to the literature, or to key items of evidence on which the experts are required to express a view, it is advisable to produce a tabbed and paginated bundle for the experts in advance of the joint meeting. Agendas should be agreed wherever possible. It is advisable to seek the experts' views on any draft agenda to ensure that all relevant topics have been covered.

# GLOSSARY

| | |
|---|---|
| **Bacteraemia** | A serious infection caused when bacteria enters the bloodstream |
| **Bacterial meningitis** | An infection of the meninges caused by bacteria (most commonly pneumococcus or meningococcus) |
| **Blood-brain barrier** | The semi-permeable membrane separating the blood from the cerebrospinal fluid |
| **Bradycardia** | Slower than normal heartrate |
| **Cerebrospinal fluid** | The fluid that surrounds the brain and the spinal cord |
| **Coagulation cascade** | The bodily reaction that leads to the formation of fibrin, a fibrous protein involved in the clotting process |
| **Cyanosis** | Bluish appearance or discolouration caused by hypoxia or lack of oxygenation |
| **Cytokinaemia** | The presence of cytokines in the blood |
| **Cytokines** | Cell signalling chemicals released by the body to fight, mediate and regulate immunity, inflammation and blood cell production. There are both pro-inflammatory cytokines and anti-inflammatory cytokines. In severe sepsis, pro-inflammatory cytokines cause capillary leakage, tissue damage and organ failure |
| **Endothelial lining** | The lining of blood vessels |
| **Endotoxins** | The part of the outer membrane of the cell wall of gram-negative bacteria |

| | |
|---|---|
| **Hypotension** | Low blood pressure (90/60mmHg or less in adults) |
| **Hypothermia** | A dangerous drop in body temperature below 35°C |
| **Hypoxia** | Where tissue is not sufficiently oxygenated |
| **Interferons** | A type of cytokine typically released by a virus-infected host cell which then prompts nearby host cells to increase their anti-viral defences |
| **Leucocytosis** | An increase in the number of white blood cells |
| **Leucopoenia** | A reduction in the number of white blood cells |
| **Meninges** | The membranes that envelop the brain and the spinal cord. The cranial meninges comprise of three membranes lying between the skull bone and the cerebrum. Immediately below the skull is the first of these, the dura mater. Below that is the arachnoid mater. Between the arachnoid mater and the pia mater (the third membrane) is the subarachnoid space, containing blood vessels and cerebrospinal fluid (CSF) |
| **Meningism** | Stiff neck, photophobia (sensitivity to light) and headache |
| **Meningitis** | Inflammation of the meninges and especially of the pia matter and arachnoid matter |
| **Meningococcus** | (aka Neisseria meningitidis). A bacterium carried in the nasopharynx, and one of the primary causes of meningitis |
| **Metabolic acidosis** | Reduced oxygen in the blood leading to chemical reactions that produce acid in the bloodstream |

| | |
|---|---|
| **Organ failure** | Where an organ ceases to perform its expected function and fails. Commonly caused by sepsis or septic shock, due to reduced blood flow such that essential nutrients are unable to reach the organs |
| **Parenteral** | Administered or occurring other than in or by the mouth |
| **Paresis** | Muscular weakness caused by nerve damage or disease |
| **Perfusion** | The passage of fluid (including blood) through the circulatory or lymphatic system |
| **Petechiae** | Pinpoint non-blanching spots |
| **Phagocyte** | White cells that can engulf and destroy pathogens including bacteria and damaged or dead cells |
| **Photophobia** | Sensitivity to light |
| **Pneumococcus** | (aka. streptococcus pneumoniae) A bacterium carried in the nasopharynx of a large portion of the population, especially children and young people, and one of the primary causes of meningitis |
| **Purpura** | Non-blanching spots of greater than 2mm |
| **Purpura fulminans** | An acute thrombotic disorder where there is loss of peripheral tissues through gangrene as a result of lack of blood flow and disturbance of the coagulation system |
| **Sepsis** | Potentially life-threatening overactive inflammatory response to severe infection |

| | |
|---|---|
| **Septicaemia** | A severe infection of the blood caused by bacteria |
| **Septic shock** | In adults, this is characterised by low blood pressure despite adequate fluid replacement, and organ dysfunction or failure, caused by over-dilation of the blood vessels. In children septic shock is sepsis with cardiovascular organ dysfunction |
| **Shock** | The life-threatening failure of adequate oxygen delivery to the tissues, which may be caused by decreased blood supply, inadequate blood oxygen saturations, or increased oxygen demand. It can lead to organ failure and death |
| **Tachycardia** | Abnormally rapid heartrate |
| **Tachypnoea** | Abnormally rapid breathing |
| **Toxic shock syndrome (TSS)** | A rare but life-threatening condition caused by bacteria getting into the body and releasing toxins |
| **Vasopressors** | Medications that cause blood vessels to contract, raising blood pressure. Also known as inotropes |

# BIBLIOGRAPHY

<u>Articles</u>

BBC News (author unaccredited), 'Sepsis test could show results 'in minutes' 19 February 2019, https://www.bbc.co.uk/news/health-47279072

Bloch-Budzier, S 'Hospital sepsis deaths 'jump by a third'', 3 August 2018, BBC, https://www.bbc.co.uk/news/health-45045438

Evans, Sharon S, Repasky, Elizabeth A, Fisher, Daniel T, 'Fever and the thermal regulation of immunity: the immune system feels the heat' *Nat Rev Immunol.* 2015 Jun; 15(6): 335–349. doi: 10.1038/nri3843

Fleischmann C, Scherag A, Adhikari NK, Hartog CS, Tsaganos T, Schlattmann P et al. 'Assessment of Global Incidence and Mortality of Hospital-treated Sepsis – Current Estimates and Limitations.' *Am J Respir Crit Care Med.* 2015. doi: 10.1164/rccm.201504-0781OC

Huang CY, Daniels R, Lembo A, Hartog C, O'Brien J, Heymann T, Reinhart K, Nguyen HB, 'Sepsis Survivors Engagement Project (SSEP); Life after sepsis: an international survey of survivors to understand the post-sepsis syndrome,' *International Journal for Quality in Health Care*, mzy137, https://doi.org/10.1093/intqhc/mzy137

Prescott HC, Osterholzer JJ, Langa KM, Angus DC, Iwashyna TJ. 'Late mortality after sepsis: propensity matched cohort study.' *BMJ.* 2016;353. doi:10.1136/bmj.i2375.

Rittirsch D, Flierl MA, Ward P 'Harmful Molecular Mechanisms in Sepsis' *Nature Reviews Immunology* volume 8, pages 776–787 (2008).

Shankar-Hari M, Rubenfeld GD. 'Understanding Long-Term Outcomes Following Sepsis: Implications and Challenges'. *Curr Infect Dis Rep.* 2016;18:37. doi: 10.1007/s11908-016-0544-7.

Singer M, Deutschman CS, Seymour CW et al, 'The Third International Consensus Definitions for Sepsis and Septic Shock (Sepsis-3)', *JAMA* 2016;315:801-810

Stiehm, ER, Damrosch, D. 'Factors in the prognosis of meningococcal infection. Review of 63 cases with emphasis on recognition and management of the severely ill patient'. *Journal of Paediatrics.* 1966;68(3)457-67.

Thompson MJ, Ninis N, Perera R, Mayon-White R, Phillips C, Bailey L, Harnden A, Mant D, Levin M. 'Clinical recognition of meningococcal disease in children and adolescents.' *Lancet.* 2006 Feb 4;367(9508):397-403. DOI: 10.1016/S0140-6736(06)67932-4

## Books

*Judicial College Guidelines for the Assessment of General Damages in Personal Injury Cases* (14th Edition, 2017), Oxford University Press.

## Other

Ninis N, Nadel S, Glennie L, *Lessons from research for doctors in training*, Meningitis Research Foundation, 4th Edition, https://www.-meningitis.org/getmedia/b412de9f-8fa4-494d-8b9f-abfb065bf654/Lessons-from-research-for-doctors-in-training-September-2018

'Meningitis (bacterial) and meningococcal septicaemia in under 16s: recognition, diagnosis and management', NICE Guideline [CG102], Published June 2010, Last updated February 2015, © NICE 2010, available from https://www.nice.org.uk/guidance/cg102 subject to https://www.nice.org.uk/terms-and-conditions#notice-of-rights. NICE guidance is prepared for the National Health Service in England. All NICE guidance is subject to regular review and may be updated or withdrawn. NICE accepts no responsibility for the use of its content in this product/publication.

'Never Events' list: https://improvement.nhs.uk/documents/2899/Never_Events_list_2018_FINAL_v6.pdf

'Sepsis: recognition, diagnosis and early management', NICE Guideline [NG51], Published July 2016, © NICE 2016, available from https://www.nice.org.uk/guidance/ng51/resources subject to https://www.nice.org.uk/terms-and-conditions#notice-of-rights. NICE guidance is prepared for the National Health Service in England. All NICE guidance is subject to regular review and may be updated or withdrawn. NICE accepts no responsibility for the use of its content in this product/publication.

# MORE BOOKS BY LAW BRIEF PUBLISHING

A selection of our other titles available now:-

| |
|---|
| 'A Practical Guide to Prison Injury Claims' by Malcolm Johnson |
| 'A Practical Guide to Hackney Carriage Licensing in London' by Stuart Jessop |
| 'A Practical Guide to Advising Clients at the Police Station' by Colin Stephen McKeown-Beaumont |
| 'A Practical Guide to Antisocial Behaviour Injunctions' by by Iain Wightwick |
| 'A Practical Guide to TOLATA Claims' by Greg Williams |
| 'Planning Obligations Demystified: A Practical Guide to Planning Obligations and Section 106 Agreements' by Bob Mc Geady & Meyric Lewis |
| 'A Practical Guide to Agricultural Law and Tenancies' by Christopher McNall |
| 'A Practical Guide to Crofting Law' by Brian Inkster |
| 'A Practical Guide to Spousal Maintenance' by Liz Cowell |
| 'A Practical Guide to the Law of Domain Names and Cybersquatting' by Andrew Clemson |
| 'A Practical Guide to the Law of Gender Pay Gap Reporting' by Harini Iyengar |
| 'Ellis and Kevan on Credit Hire – 5th Edition' by Aidan Ellis & Tim Kevan |
| 'Artificial Intelligence – The Practical Legal Issues' by John Buyers |
| 'A Practical Guide to the Rights of Grandparents in Children Proceedings' by Stuart Barlow |
| 'NHS Whistleblowing and the Law' by Joseph England |
| 'Employment Law and the Gig Economy' by Nigel Mackay & Annie Powell |
| 'A Practical Guide to the General Data Protection Regulation (GDPR)' by Keith Markham |
| 'A Practical Guide to Noise Induced Hearing Loss (NIHL) Claims' by Andrew Mckie, Ian Skeate, Gareth McAloon |

'An Introduction to Beauty Negligence Claims – A Practical Guide for the Personal Injury Practitioner' by Greg Almond

'Intercompany Agreements for Transfer Pricing Compliance' by Paul Sutton

'Zen and the Art of Mediation' by Martin Plowman

'A Practical Guide to the SRA Principles, Individual and Law Firm Codes of Conduct 2019 – What Every Law Firm Needs to Know' by Paul Bennett

'A Practical Guide to Licensing Law for Commercial Property Lawyers' by Niall McCann & Richard Williams

'A Practical Guide to Adoption for Family Lawyers' by Graham Pegg

'Essential Motor Finance Law for the Busy Practitioner' by Richard Humphreys

'A Practical Guide to Industrial Disease Claims' by Andrew Mckie & Ian Skeate

'A Practical Guide to the Law of Armed Conflict' by Jo Morris & Libby Anderson

'A Practical Guide to Redundancy' by Philip Hyland

'A Practical Guide to Vicarious Liability' by Mariel Irvine

'A Practical Guide to Claims Arising from Delays in Diagnosing Cancer' by Bella Webb

'A Practical Guide to Applications for Landlord's Consent and Variation of Leases' by Mark Shelton

'A Practical Guide to Relief from Sanctions Post-Mitchell and Denton' by Peter Causton

'Butler's Equine Tax Planning: 2nd Edition' by Julie Butler

'A Practical Guide to Equity Release for Advisors' by Paul Sams

'A Practical Guide to Unlawful Eviction and Harassment' by Stephanie Lovegrove

'A Practical Guide to the Law Relating to Food' by Ian Thomas

'A Practical Guide to the Ending of Assured Shorthold Tenancies' by Elizabeth Dwomoh

'A Practical Guide to Financial Services Claims' by Chris Hegarty

'The Law of Houses in Multiple Occupation: A Practical Guide to HMO Proceedings' by Julian Hunt

'A Practical Guide to Unlawful Eviction and Harassment' by Stephanie Lovegrove

'A Practical Guide to Solicitor and Client Costs' by Robin Dunne

'A Practical Guide to Wrongful Conception, Wrongful Birth and Wrongful Life Claims' by Rebecca Greenstreet

'Occupiers, Highways and Defective Premises Claims: A Practical Guide Post-Jackson – 2nd Edition' by Andrew Mckie

'A Practical Guide to Financial Ombudsman Service Claims' by Adam Temple & Robert Scrivenor

'A Practical Guide to the Law of Enfranchisement and Lease Extension' by Paul Sams

'A Practical Guide to Marketing for Lawyers – 2nd Edition' by Catherine Bailey & Jennet Ingram

'A Practical Guide to Advising Schools on Employment Law' by Jonathan Holden

'Certificates of Lawful Use and Development: A Guide to Making and Determining Applications' by Bob Mc Geady & Meyric Lewis

'A Practical Guide to the Law of Dilapidations' by Mark Shelton

'A Guide to Consent in Clinical Negligence Post-Montgomery' by Lauren Sutherland QC

'A Practical Guide to Running Housing Disrepair and Cavity Wall Claims: 2nd Edition' by Andrew Mckie & Ian Skeate

'A Practical Guide to Digital and Social Media Law for Lawyers' by Sherree Westell

'A Practical Guide to Holiday Sickness Claims – 2nd Edition' by Andrew Mckie & Ian Skeate

'A Practical Guide to Elderly Law' by Justin Patten

'Arguments and Tactics for Personal Injury and Clinical Negligence Claims' by Dorian Williams

'A Practical Guide to QOCS and Fundamental Dishonesty' by James Bentley

'A Practical Guide to Drone Law' by Rufus Ballaster, Andrew Firman, Eleanor Clot

'Practical Mediation: A Guide for Mediators, Advocates, Advisers, Lawyers, and Students in Civil, Commercial, Business, Property, Workplace, and Employment Cases' by Jonathan Dingle with John Sephton

'A Practical Guide to Compliance for Personal Injury Firms Working With Claims Management Companies' by Paul Bennett

'A Practical Guide to the Landlord and Tenant Act 1954: Commercial Tenancies' by Richard Hayes & David Sawtell

'A Practical Guide to Psychiatric Claims in Personal Injury' by Liam Ryan

| ‘A Practical Guide to Dog Law for Owners and Others’ by Andrea Pitt |
|---|
| ‘RTA Allegations of Fraud in a Post-Jackson Era: The Handbook – 2nd Edition’ by Andrew Mckie |
| ‘RTA Personal Injury Claims: A Practical Guide Post-Jackson’ by Andrew Mckie |
| ‘On Experts: CPR35 for Lawyers and Experts’ by David Boyle |
| ‘An Introduction to Personal Injury Law’ by David Boyle |
| ‘A Practical Guide to Claims Arising From Accidents Abroad and Travel Claims’ by Andrew Mckie & Ian Skeate |
| ‘A Practical Guide to Chronic Pain Claims’ by Pankaj Madan |
| ‘A Practical Guide to Claims Arising from Fatal Accidents’ by James Patience |
| ‘A Practical Approach to Clinical Negligence Post-Jackson’ by Geoffrey Simpson-Scott |
| ‘Employers' Liability Claims: A Practical Guide Post-Jackson’ by Andrew Mckie |
| ‘A Practical Guide to Subtle Brain Injury Claims’ by Pankaj Madan |
| ‘The Law of Driverless Cars: An Introduction’ by Alex Glassbrook |
| ‘A Practical Guide to Costs in Personal Injury Cases’ by Matthew Hoe |
| ‘The No Nonsense Solicitors’ Practice: A Guide To Running Your Firm’ by Bettina Brueggemann |
| ‘The Queen's Counsel Lawyer's Omnibus: 20 Years of Cartoons from The Times 1993-2013’ by Alex Steuart Williams |

These books and more are available to order online direct from the publisher at www.lawbriefpublishing.com, where you can also read free sample chapters. For any queries, contact us on 0844 587 2383 or mail@lawbriefpublishing.com.

Our books are also usually in stock at www.amazon.co.uk with free next day delivery for Prime members, and at good legal bookshops such as Wildy & Sons.

We are regularly launching new books in our series of practical day-to-day practitioners' guides. Visit our website and join our free newsletter to be kept informed and to receive special offers, free chapters, etc.

You can also follow us on Twitter at www.twitter.com/lawbriefpub.

# INDEX

## A



## B



## C

# D



# E



# F



# G



# H



# I

# J



# L



# M



# N

# O



# P



# R



# S



# T

# V



# W

www.ingramcontent.com/pod-product-compliance
Lightning Source LLC
LaVergne TN
LVHW022106200926
848481LV00003B/1072
*9781912687299*